A Passage from Solitude

A Passage from Solitude
Training the Mind in a Life Embracing the World

A modern commentary on Tibetan Buddhist Mind Training

by B. Alan Wallace
Edited by Zara Houshmand

Snow Lion Publications
Ithaca, New York USA

Snow Lion Publications
P.O. Box 6483
Ithaca, New York 14851
USA

Copyright © 1992 B. Alan Wallace

First Edition U.S.A. 1992

Printed in the USA

ISBN 1-55939-005-0

Library of Congress Cataloging-in-Publication Data

Wallace, B. Alan.
    A passage from solitude : training the mind in a life embracing
the world : a modern commentary on Tibetan Buddhist mind training /
by B. Alan Wallace ; edited by Zara Houshmand.
        p.   cm.
    Includes bibliographical references.
    ISBN 1-55939-005-0
    1. Spiritual life—Buddhism.   2. Buddhism—China—Tibet-
-Doctrines.   I. Houshmand, Zara.   II. Title.
BQ7805.W35   1992
294.3'444—dc20   92-15849
                                                            CIP

Contents

Introduction

In our search for the meaning of life, we may overlook the fact that life doesn't necessarily have any meaning at all. The meaning of life is not presented to us, but is something that we create ourselves. In the third chapter of the *Dhammapada* the Buddha says, "As a fletcher makes straight his arrow, a wise man makes straight his trembling and unsteady thought, which is difficult to guard, difficult to hold back."[1] In this society with its hurly-burly pace demanding of our time, it is ever so easy to let life slip by. Looking back after ten, twenty, thirty years, we wonder what we have really accomplished. We have made so much money per year and spent so much again. We have bought new clothes and worn them out, eaten and defecated, experienced sickness and health. This process of simply existing is not necessarily meaningful. And yet, there is an unlimited potential for meaning and value in this human existence. The Seven-Point Mind Training is one eminently practical way of tapping into that meaning.

The tradition of the Seven-Point Mind Training can be traced back to Atīśa who received these teachings from Serlingpa (gSer gling pa) roughly one thousand years ago. The tradition passed

[1] *Dhammapada*, III, 33. Trans. F. Max Muller, Sacred Books of the East, Vol.10. Reprinted, AVF Books Distributors, Delhi, 1987.

orally to Chekawa ('Chad kha ba), who wrote down the verses of the root text preserved here. The oral transmission of the practice has continued unbroken to the present, and I received it in 1973 from the Tibetan lay teacher Ku-ngo Barshi.

At the time I had recently become a monk, and was attending the Buddhist School of Dialectics in Dharamsala. I had lived for a while at the Tibetan Medical Center where Ku-ngo Barshi was the chief instructor; he and his wife lived in a very small wooden shack nearby. He was an extremely learned man, a scholar of Buddhist philosophy and logic, as well as Tibetan medicine, astrology, poetry, and grammar. But I was impressed as much by his humility, serenity, and good cheer, as by his erudition.

He was from an aristocratic family in Tibet, and had experienced first-hand the great tragedy inflicted on his homeland when the Chinese communists took over. He fled with his wife to India, but some of his family members stayed behind and had suffered greatly. Later when I got to know him well, he told me that the Chinese had in fact done him a great service. In Tibet, although devoted to the Dharma, he said he had been complacent and somewhat lax in his practice. The hardships he experienced in exile had given him insight into the nature of suffering that enhanced the depth and quality of his motivation for practicing Dharma.

The serenity, humility, and good cheer of this man, then in his sixties, proved his point, and I was honored to be taught by him: at the heart of the Seven-Point Mind Training lies this transformation of the circumstances that life brings us, however hard, as the raw material from which we create our own spiritual path.

Fourteen years after I had received the teachings from Ku-ngo Barshi, I taught on the Seven-Point Mind Training during a nine-month retreat near Lone Pine in the eastern Sierra Nevada mountains in California. It was October, 1987, when I finished recording the series of talks on which this book is based, which I sent to interested friends in Seattle, Washington at their request. This was an auspicious time of blue skies and cool breezes, when the willows and locust trees turned to colors of fire. After fourteen years as a Buddhist monk, I had recently returned my monastic vows to re-enter lay life, and these were the first teachings I gave as a lay person. The Seven-Point Mind Training was especially meaningful for this transition.

I have entitled this book *A Passage from Solitude* for two reasons. First, its contents, like passages from a journal, are my reflections while dwelling in the solitudes of the high California desert. Secondly, the central theme of the Seven-Point Mind Training is to make the liberating passage from the constricting solitude of self-centeredness to the warm kinship with others which occurs with the cultivation of cherishing others even more than oneself.

This Mind Training is especially well suited for an active life. It does not require that we withdraw in seclusion, but that we re-examine all of our relationships—to family, friends, enemies, and strangers—and gradually transform our responses to whatever life throws our way. It is a Mahāyāna practice that aspires to attain full awakening through compassion and loving kindness for all creatures.

The term *Mind Training* is a literal rendering of the Tibetan *lo jong (blo sbyong)*. The word *lo* can be translated as *mind, attitude, way of thinking,* or *mind state.* But Tibetan makes no distinction between the mind and heart, so the word applies equally to the feelings of the heart. Accurately speaking, the Seven-Point Mind/Heart Training entails a change of heart as much as a transformation of the mind.

The root text of the Seven-Point Mind Training,[2] as recorded by Chekawa, is so concise as to be extremely obscure, but it was never meant to be self-explanatory. The verses, brief enough to be easily memorized, are intended to serve as a mnemonic device for the commentary. After hearing the teachings as oral commentary, or in the surrogate form that a book such as this can offer, then as you recite the verses, hopefully

---

[2]The Table of Contents gives this root text by itself.

the full meaning comes flooding in from memory. Memoriz-
ing a text such as this can help greatly in putting the teachings into practice; whereas, if our knowledge is confined to
the pages, it remains on the shelf with the book, easily for-
gotten when we are caught up in the affairs of daily life.

The commentary serves as a series of guided meditations,
alternating with suggestions for sustaining in our active life
the insights reached through meditation. Treat it as a work-
book, not as something to finish in one reading.

In addition to the oral tradition received from Ku-ngo Barshi, I have used two other commentaries as the background
for my own. One is possibly the most ancient commentary on
this text that still exists, and yet it remains very useful today.
It consists of notes taken during Chekawa's own oral discourses
on the Mind Training by a little-known disciple of his named
Sechibuwa (Se spyil bu ba). It is not available in translation,
so I will share many of Sechibuwa's suggestions, which
presumably were inspired by Chekawa himself. The other is
among the most recent of contemporary commentaries, found
in the excellent book called *Advice from a Spiritual Friend,* by
Geshe Rabten and Geshe Dhargyey.[3] This is actually a tran-
scription of discourses given by my principal teacher, Geshe
Rabten, which I had missed. I had therefore turned to Ku-
ngo Barshi for these teachings. As the cycle continues, I hope
I have also added something that may especially be of value
from the viewpoint of the West.

The order of the verses in Geshe Rabten's book varies from
that used here; there are likewise many differences of interpretation between the various commentaries, and between the
Mind Training and other teachings. Readers familiar with the
stages of the path presented in *Lam Rim* teachings,[4] for example, will notice that the Mind Training differs significantly in

[3]Published by Wisdom Publications, London, 1984.

[4]There are now a number of *Lam Rim* treatises available in English translation, but the primary source of them all is Atīśa's *Bodhipathapradipa,*
translated as *A Lamp for the Path to Enlightenment* in the volume *Atisha
in Tibet,* by A. Chattopadhya and Lama Chinpa, Calcutta, 1976.

both emphasis and sequence. Such differences should not cause consternation. It is commonly said in Tibet that "each lama has his own Dharma." Each teacher is unique, as are the needs of each student, and there is room within the teachings to accommodate these differences.

This touches on an issue I would like to address before beginning with the text, that of the relationship between *guru* and disciple. What does it mean to enter into such a relationship, and what does the commitment entail?

In choosing a spiritual mentor, if we make that choice, it would be misguided to seek out the teacher with the greatest reputation, the highest status, or the most disciples. Rather, we are well advised to seek the person from whom we receive the greatest blessings. What does this mean? By contact with this person, by simply being with him and conversing with him, we find our mind transformed in a wholesome way. Another teacher, perhaps even someone more knowledgeable and with deeper insight, may not bring about the change of mind and heart that this person's words, presence, and teachings bring to us. The spiritual guide we choose should be someone we trust very deeply, because in essence our commitment is one of trust. It is extremely helpful in our progress on the path to see this person as our chief source of reliance, and his advice to us as the central pillar of our practice.

The relationship need not, and should not, be exclusive. Think of the root guru as the tap root that provides the central source of nourishment for the growth of the plant. Other subsidiary roots may feed into it, picking up minerals or water from sources that the tap root does not reach. Nevertheless, the nourishment of the plant comes chiefly from the tap root, and all of the subsidiary roots are understood within its context. If we feel so inclined, it is well worthwhile to learn from other teachers, even from other traditions. His Holiness the Dalai Lama, for instance, has received teachings from teachers trained in various traditions, including the Gelug order and the Nyingma order. And when he first came to the West, he said that the reason for his coming was not to teach, but to learn from the wise men of the West.

Such diversity enriches the teachings of one's root guru, and throws greater light upon them. It also helps to avoid the bigotry and muddle-headed sectarianism implied in the attitude that one's own teacher is superior to all others. Personality cults, or adoration of a guru's charisma, are inappropriate in the context of Buddhism. This is not to deny the affection and respect we feel towards our teachers, or the delight in their presence; but intense emotional attachment is out of tune with the melody of the Buddhadharma.

You may have heard the saying, "Rely not on the person, rely on the teachings." The ultimate source of reliance is the Dharma itself. The guru may serve as a doctor, but the teachings are the medicine that actually makes us well. The doctor is there to administer the medicine, to reveal the path to awakening, to aid in the healing process.

The guru/disciple relationship should also be continually balanced by an emphasis on our own Buddha nature. This is known as fruitional refuge, a reliance on the awakened being that we ourselves will become. This self-reliance and cultivation of our own wisdom is essential; there are, and should be, many times when our spiritual mentor is not available, and we *must* be our own guru. The external guru serves to aid us in unveiling our own Buddha nature, so that our innate wisdom can shine forth ever more clearly.

In conclusion, I would like to express my deep gratitude first to Pauly and Werner Fitze for transcribing the recorded lectures on which this book is based; and I am very grateful to Zara Houshmand for her excellent work in editing those transcripts, without which this book would likely never have appeared.

Although no book, or even tape recording, can replace a direct oral transmission, I hope you benefit from the teaching that follows, because this is the whole point. If you enter the practice and do your best, with perseverance and continuity, and still find that you do not benefit, then I suggest that you switch to something that is effective. The core of Dharma practice is to find whatever works to bring about a more wholesome way of life. It can provide an eternal wellspring of joy in our lives that allows us to be more and more effective in relieving the distress of others and bringing them to a state of greater contentment and well-being.

The First Point
The Preliminaries,
Which Are Fundamental Dharma

First of all train in the preliminaries.

Of the two commentaries to this text mentioned previously, by Sechibuwa and Geshe Rabten, the former interprets the preliminaries as the stages of the Lam Rim practices commonly taught in Tibetan Buddhism.[1]

Geshe Rabten, however, gives a more modest interpretation of "preliminaries," and one that has precedents in other commentaries. He stresses a familiarity with four points, the most fundamental facets of the Lam Rim: an awareness of the preciousness of human life, of death and impermanence, of *karma* and the effects of karma, and of the unsatisfactory nature of the cycle of existence.

With these four points as a solid foundation, fundamental to any kind of Buddhist practice, we are well equipped to enter the Seven-Point Mind Training, which is very much a Mahāyāna practice. Let's look briefly at the four points.

---

[1]See H.H. the Dalai Lama, Tenzin Gyatso, *Path to Bliss,* trans. Geshe Thubten Jinpa, ed. Christine Cox (Ithaca, N.Y.: Snow Lion Publications, 1991).

1.   THE PRECIOUSNESS OF HUMAN LIFE

In this lifetime, each of us is gifted with a human body and with circumstances, both external and internal, that are conducive to a fruitful spiritual practice of potentially great depth. To understand how precious this opportunity is, it helps to have reached a sense of conviction that we are each endowed with a continuum of consciousness that is not confined to this life alone, and, moreover, that our actions and behavior have significance from one life to another.

This is not to brush aside any qualms or uncertainties that may surround the issues of reincarnation and karma. If you seriously question the continuity of awareness from life to life, I encourage you to investigate this both in practice and in theory[2]—not with a leap of blind faith but with all your intelligence.

If you have worked through this and reached an understanding that we do indeed participate in a flow of consciousness that came before this life and will continue after, then extend this understanding into the past, life before life through time out of mind, and reflect on where this sequence of lives without beginning has led. The answer, of course, is to this moment right now: Here I am, for better and for worse, with the wholesome qualities I have cultivated and the mental distortions that still afflict me. Here I am, the fruition of the infinite past. Once we have gained the confidence of conviction in this area, it is so beneficial, and so awe-inspiring, to weave this awareness into our consciousness and let it permeate our subtle emotional responses, our deepest sense of who we are.

Given that our minds are indestructible and without beginning, but are shaped by our behavior and bear the fruit of our actions, what is worth doing with our lives? Unless we have integrated the awareness of past and future lives into our way of viewing the world, our values and our life decisions

---

[2]For a modern explanation of the Buddhist theory of continuity of consciousness from one life to another see my *Choosing Reality: A Contemplative View of Physics and the Mind* (Boston: Shambhala, 1989), chapter 23, "A Contemplative View of the Mind."

are probably dominated by a sense of this current lifetime as an isolated event.

For example, we approach any major commitment by asking ourselves what we can expect out of it. What lasting effect will it have? By and large such questions are confined to this lifetime. After a week, or a month, or a year, how will this influence my life? Of course, the answer is that we cannot expect anything. We cannot know what will happen next year any more than we knew what would happen this year. It is very important not to grasp at forms, thinking that the year will be a success only if it turns out a certain way. Simply drop such expectations and remain fluid. Instead, we can work very deeply with the motivation that the year—whatever we are doing—may be of the greatest possible benefit, not only in this lifetime but overall, in service to others and in our own growth towards full awakening. The motivation is of paramount importance.

As we take into account this linear progression from past life to present to future, we can appreciate the rare and precious opportunities that this fully endowed human life presents to us right now: the gifts of our teachers, the circumstances that are conducive to practice, the countless means we have for transforming our lives in a wholesome way. From this context we can also look laterally, to other sentient beings around us. Everyone desires essentially the same things as ourselves—a lasting state of contentment and freedom from suffering, pain, anxiety, and fear.

Although this common ground we share with every sentient being in the universe is utterly simple, the ways that individuals strive to fulfill this eternal longing vary with infinite diversity. And, for so many people, these methods are pathetically ineffective. We don't need to be great sages to see that many people fail tragically at finding happiness and freeing their minds from unnecessary grief. It takes no deep insight to see that the source of both our well-being and our maladies lies within our own hearts and minds. To change our experience of life we must inevitably change our hearts and minds, or rather our heart/minds.

The Buddhadharma starts from where we are right now, with our uncertainties and our shortcomings, as well as our wholesome qualities. It starts *here*, not after we have become *bodhisattvas*. It shows a clear path for living a meaningful, wholesome life of increasing contentment and good cheer in this very lifetime, and it shows us how to sow the seeds for our well-being in future lives. If we seek to heal the mind completely of afflictions—hostility, attachment, and confusion—and to unveil our Buddha nature, allowing every wholesome potential to shine forth completely unobscured, the Buddhadharma shows us clearly and accessibly how to achieve this. And we have encountered this body of teachings for fulfilling every wholesome desire right here in this lifetime. Look to your past and recognize how utterly precious this is. How many of our companions on planet earth, striving for happiness in myriad ways, have found such a rich body of practices to transform their lives and effectively fulfill their aspirations—aspirations we share whether or not we are Buddhist? In this way we can begin to realize the preciousness of a fully endowed human life.

As this sinks in, priorities change. Before, we might have said, "The teachings are good. They are all very well, but given my job and my family, my bills, the city I live in, all my responsibilities and commitments, I just don't have time. I don't have time to hear teachings, or to meditate, or to read books on Dharma. I don't have time to bring my mind to Dharma." This suggests a set of priorities that leaves precious little time for Dharma. What could be more important? Keep in mind that Dharma is not confined to formal practice, sitting cross-legged in meditation or reciting *sadhanas*. Dharma is meant here in a broad sense; but not in a sense so diluted—or deluded—that "living Dharma all the time" means very little Dharma at all.

As we become aware of the preciousness of human life in the context of successive lifetimes, priorities shift, leading us to make various sacrifices: lesser wages, for example. There isn't anyone who is too busy to practice Dharma. There are plenty of people who have priorities that they place above Dharma.

2. DEATH AND IMPERMANENCE

An awareness of death and impermanence enhances the vivid realization of the preciousness of a fully endowed human life in a way that transforms the heart and mind. It is possible to be lethargic in a very dynamic way: lethargic in relation to Dharma but dynamic regarding *saṃsāra*. We have plenty of time for entertainment, movies, vacations, sports, and partying. We have plenty of time for work. But we have precious little time for Dharma, thinking, "Perhaps, when the kids are older, when I retire, when the work eases off a bit, or when winter comes, or summer. . . ." We always assume that there will be time later, but in the process we are aging and our vitality is waning. Impermanence means we are changing, and approaching death.

Once we have gained a sense of belief in the continuity of consciousness from lifetime to lifetime, we are in a fruitful position to meditate on the fact of our own deaths. We can accept this fact and integrate an awareness of the event into the fabric of our world view and our priorities.

This is no less true for those who have children. Parents may sacrifice time for Dharma thinking, "The children need my time," or spend hours away for the sake of a good salary. But what is the quality of the work we are doing? What is the quality of our relationship with our children and our spouse? What are we really offering, if we have so little Dharma in our lives? We may be sacrificing quality for quantity.

Meditation on death and impermanence shows that there is no time to squander. The need for Dharma is urgent. Death may be imminent for each of us, and the fact of our death is utterly certain. All mundane goals that we strive for will certainly pass, and all that will remain is the imprints: the growth derived from our Dharma practice or, on the other side of the ledger, the force of habits that are motivated by mental distortions.

3.   ACTIONS AND THEIR RESULTS

An awareness of death and impermanence leads very quickly to an investigation of the nature of actions and their results. Actions provide the coherent relationship that links one life to another. Each action leaves its imprint upon our consciousness and, sooner or later, inevitably manifests its fruit unless it has somehow been nullified by other actions. Actions need not be physical. With each phrase, each comment, and, most frightening of all, each thought, we are creating our futures for better or worse. And the present that we experience right now is what we have created by the karma of our past actions.

Merely to believe this is impotent. It accomplishes nothing to sign on the dotted line, "I am a Buddhist and this is part of the Buddhist creed." Having stumbled upon a lump of gold, it is pointless to put it away in a box. It is better to benefit from it instead: to use it in industry, make some jewelry, or exchange it for something we can enjoy. Likewise, having reached the certainty that each of our actions and its results is profoundly significant, not only within this lifetime but beyond, it is important to use this wonderful discovery. Let the understanding of karma transform our priorities, our values, our world view, and thus transform our way of life.

4.   THE UNSATISFACTORY NATURE OF THE CYCLE OF EXISTENCE

The last of the four fundamental preliminaries emphasized in Geshe Rabten's commentary is the unsatisfactory nature of the cycle of existence. The term *saṃsāra*, translated as cycle of existence, is often misused by Westerners. Even people familiar with Buddhist teachings use the term casually to refer to their physical environment, be it the planet earth or Los Angeles. This is missing the point. Saṃsāra is not a geographic location, nor is it nature. Buddhas have lived on planet earth, and yet they are utterly free of saṃsāra. Saṃsāra is a condition of life, but it is not life itself. Escaping from saṃsāra does not mean being extinguished or annihilated, any more than it means leaving the city for a mountain retreat.

The cycle of existence is a way of being. Specifically, it is the condition of being propelled from the experience of one lifetime to another by the force of our mental afflictions and the actions they have tainted. This condition of existence, and the dissatisfaction it produces, is the subject of meditation.

Why meditate on suffering? It's not much fun. There are so many more enjoyable subjects in the wonderful menu of Tibetan meditation practices, let alone in other traditions: loving kindness, soothing breath awareness, tantric sadhanas, dream yoga—for that matter, we could go to a good movie or out for a pizza! With all of this competition, why meditate on suffering? So we can escape from suffering.

There is something unsatisfying about the way we live, and this need not continue. Otherwise, the Buddha would never have troubled us by pointing out the unsatisfying nature of life—even a successful life, a delightful family situation, a good job, a sunny day. Why is there an element of dissatisfaction and anxiety in all human relations, lying so often just beneath the surface, even in times of pleasure? Something is awry, but the fault is not outside us in the environment. Saṃsāra is not out *there*, but rather in the way that we experience our environment. To target it precisely, saṃsāra is in the quality of our minds. Our minds are not functioning in accord with reality, and therein lies the problem.

The Lam Rim teachings on the stages of the path elaborate on the various types of suffering. It is important to spend some time on this, whether we are old hands at Buddhadharma or have recently encountered it.[3] The New Age movement has emphasized the power of affirmative thinking: focusing on the positive aspects of our lives can reinforce or help to realize them. This could imply that meditation on suffering increases the

---

[3]See, for example, Geshe Rabten's *Treasury of Dharma: A Tibetan Buddhist Meditation Course,* trans. Gonsar Rinpoche, ed. Brian Grabia (London: Tharpa Publications, 1988), pp. 14-20.

experience of suffering. If we practice incorrectly, this can be quite true. I have met very sincere Buddhists—usually Western Buddhists—who walk about in a cloud of pessimistic gloom and doom that they have created in their meditations. Their enjoyment of something as simple as ice cream is soured by the notion that everything is suffering. This response to life is a distortion of the practice. On the other hand, people who have spent a great deal of time in Lam Rim meditations on suffering and its sources tend to be cheerful, serene, and contented as a result.

I once translated for a Tibetan lama who spoke to a large group about the different types of suffering that we experience. When it was time for questions, a member of the audience asked, "Lama, you have been speaking at such length about all these forms of suffering and the fact that all of our experience is permeated by dissatisfaction. Yet, while teaching this, both you and your interpreter seemed so happy. How can you talk so cheerfully about suffering?"

The lama paused and then responded, with a big smile, "There is such a thing as untainted joy." By this he meant joy untainted by the mental afflictions of attachment, anger, or confusion. Why meditate on suffering? So that we can escape it and discover, gradually through our own experience, the contentment that arises from a wholesome and balanced heart and mind. What can prod us to cultivate this quality of awareness from day to day, from moment to moment? A vivid awareness that investing our lives in the acquisition of pleasant external stimuli results only in dissatisfaction.

What it would take to be really happy? Do we think of a change in our environment, relationships, acquisitions, or health? Or do we answer instead, "If my heart and mind were more loving, if I were free of resentment, more forgiving, more fluid in my responses to life, endowed with greater wisdom and mental stability. . . ."

Meditation on suffering holds enormous practical value and is a necessary foundation for making full use of the Seven-Point Mind Training. Many Buddhist teachers have emphasized the need for deep insight into the nature of suffering in order to develop true compassion and loving kindness towards other living beings. Otherwise compassion arises only when we see someone in obvious pain. When we see the bland, expressionless faces of people walking down the street, we may feel nothing much at all and think, "So what? They are living their lives and I am living mine." But if we look deeper, with vivid awareness, into the actual nature of our existence, the source of happiness and suffering, the role of karma, the fact of impermanence and of death, and the precious value of a fully endowed human life, then a much deeper sense of compassion for other beings can arise and endure. Only this compassion can form the basis for *bodhicitta*, the spirit of awakening.

The Second Point
The Main Practice: Training in the Bodhicittas

Directly or implicitly, the entire Seven-Point Mind Training deals with the cultivation of the two bodhicittas: ultimate bodhicitta that probes the nature of reality to realize its emptiness, and relative bodhicitta that aspires to attain full awakening out of compassion and loving kindness for all creatures. This second point of the training includes both of these aspirations, beginning first with ultimate bodhicitta.

THE CULTIVATION OF ULTIMATE BODHICITTA

Having attained stability, let the mystery be revealed.

The verse introducing the second point identifies stability as a prerequisite for receiving the secret teachings. Before we can fruitfully investigate the nature of ultimate reality, it may be helpful to speak of two types of stability that are necessary: existential and theoretical.

Although *existential* is a Western term, it is meaningful in the context of Buddhadharma. If we are living with major psychological problems or experiencing an inner crisis of insecurity, if we have fundamental doubts about the meaning of life, if we suffer from very strong anger or attachment, these may be deemed existential issues. They concern the way we exist and the quality of our minds. Any kind of major psychological imbalance indicates a lack of existential stability. We are well advised first to put our house in order on this mundane level, before probing the depths of the ultimate nature of reality.

What are the indications of existential stability? Mental balance is felt as a sense of contentment, recognizing our own mental afflictions and knowing how to attenuate them gradually. A genuine sense of refuge is also extremely important. In investigating the ultimate nature of reality, we are entering unexplored territory. The experience can be frightening, even terrifying. The more deeply we delve into the nature of our own personal identity and of external reality, the more important it is to have a real sense of trust in the teachings themselves, in their source, the Buddha Śākyamuni, as well as in the spiritual friends who guide us on the path.

It is worthwhile examining the difficulty, so common in the West, of integrating this sense of refuge with a reliance upon the full power of our own intelligence and innate wisdom. The scientist in us, the critical thinker, levels the finger, saying: "You Buddhists, Christians, followers of religion, have bound yourselves to one creed and are afraid to entertain any thought that may conflict with your doctrine. You have blinded yourselves and are not free to investigate reality." This is no easy criticism to shrug off, as it often contains an element of truth. But it is not the final word.

To study science we need confidence. Physics itself, the most fundamental of the hard sciences, demands our confidence in certain axioms—that the universe obeys mathematical laws, that the world behind appearances is coherent and accessible to our intellect. Without these assumptions we cannot play the game. Further, if we lack faith in the scientific method and the immense body of previous experimentation, there is no way that we can engage in original research. If we doubt the integrity of generations of physicists before us, suspecting that the results of their experiments were distorted by such motives as profit, rivalry, or hope of tenure, we would then need to reproduce for ourselves the work of Newton, Kepler, Galileo, and others before them, checking all their mathematics. Then, are the mathematics really sound? We would have to test Pythagoras....

Clearly, one cannot be a physicist without faith. It requires the full force of intelligence, but intelligence can function to its fullest only when we base it on a deep sense of faith. This is as true of Buddhism as it is of physics. The exercise of intelligence and the cultivation of faith are mutually compatible and enhance each other richly. It is also true that blind faith hampers the growth of wisdom. If we allow ourselves to be complacent and settle for a leap of faith instead of understanding, the critic has the right to question the findings of our investigation of reality.

But placing our trust in Buddhist teachings, or a Buddhist teacher, or in the Buddha himself, does not mean putting on blinkers. Taking refuge is not an act of blind faith. It is based on our intelligence and understanding, but also goes beyond these. The knowledge that we have acquired in this lifetime is so utterly minute in comparison with the reality that surrounds us that we would be terribly constricted if we were to base our actions strictly on our present knowledge; because essentially we know nothing of what will happen five minutes from now, let alone a year or fifty years. While our knowledge has very definite demarcations, faith does not.

A common analogy compares the blessings received from awakened beings to the sun shining down on the earth. A mind that has faith is like a cup turned upwards, and the sunlight floods into it. Nothing happens to the sun; we simply become accessible to a fantastic enrichment of our lives. As the blessings pour in, they nourish our lives, enhancing and cultivating wisdom. Wisdom in turn gives rise to greater faith, which in turn provides a broader foundation for the growth of wisdom. But lacking faith, our minds are closed to growth, not venturing beyond what we have already understood.

Existential stability includes this sense of faith. But the cultivation of ultimate bodhicitta also requires what I would call theoretical stability, a firm grounding in conventional truth. Before looking deeply into the question of emptiness as taught in the Madhyamaka, or Centrist, tradition, we must have a sound, though not necessarily elaborate, understanding of the significance of actions and their results, the relationship of virtue and non-virtue to well-being and dis-ease. It is critically important to understand that these major facets of relative truth are in no way undermined by the teachings on emptiness.

According to the Madhyamaka view, all phenomena exist as dependently related events. Because phenomena—including myself, you, and our communication here—exist as dependently related events, each of these phenomena is for this very reason devoid of an intrinsic identity. Each of these entities does not truly exist inasmuch as it has no existence as an isolated, solitary, self-existent phenomenon. Rather, each one exists only as a dependently related event.

Having attained stability, let the mystery be revealed. The teachings on śūnyatā, or emptiness, are called a mystery because they are not evident to the senses. We cannot experience this view of reality by simply gazing about us and observing appearances, because the ultimate mode of our existence—of our selves, our bodies, our environment—is contrary to how it appears. Although it is mysterious in this sense, nevertheless it can be experienced, and this experience radically transforms the mind.

Consider the world as dreamlike.

With this verse the author enters into the meditation and the unfolding of the mystery. Consider the world as if it were a dream. The commentary explains that this refers to the apprehended world of phenomena. In other words, start from what you observe and regard it as being dreamlike. I am looking now over the Owens Valley and the sky is a shade of purple and pink. In the dusk the sage grows darker, and the mountains across the valley also grow dark. These are the objects, the environment, that I observe.

What does "dreamlike" mean here? If we understand it superficially to mean unreal or dreamy in a vague, unfocused
sense, we miss the whole point. Other analogies may serve as
well: the apprehended world is compared to a mirage, a mag-
ical illusion, an echo, or a reflection in a mirror. But a dream
is especially apt.

Think back to an actual dream, a vivid one. While we dream,
the events in the dream seem really to be happening: we find
ourselves on another continent, a conversation takes place, we
are punished or rewarded, perhaps even die. Anything can happen. All the appearances are there. But in spite of appearances,
no such events are occurring. A woman dreams that she gives
birth to a child, the child grows up, then is killed, and the
woman grieves. She has experienced the whole process, but
wakes up to recognize that there was no birth, no child, no
death. In this sense phenomena are dreamlike: there is no substantial reality that accords with appearances. We observe
phenomena as being far more concrete and tangible than in
fact they are, and this is misleading. It occurs because of the
mental process of reification.

Sechibuwa explains that there is no entity apart from the
mind that is anything more than a deceptive appearance to
the mind. Nothing exists independently of consciousness or
mental designation. At first glance this looks like idealism, a
denial of external reality: everything is just of the stuff of the
mind. At this point, those of us grounded in the scientific view
should be raising our eyebrows. Can we seriously accept that
there is no substantial reality? Einstein said that the belief in
an external world, existing in its own right and following natural laws, is fundamental to all science. Are we now throwing
out the foundations underlying all of Western science? In a
sense we are.

Some of the most recent research in physics, especially in
fundamental areas such as quantum mechanics and relativity,
severely questions the traditional notion of a "real" world behind the veil of appearances and perceptions. The classical par-

adigm of atoms bouncing off each other in absolute time and space is rejected, at least when physicists are thinking most critically. Unfortunately, this insight has had very little impact on the other sciences. But physicists who are concerned with the fundamental reality of physics and not simply the practical applications cannot scoff at philosophical questions. Reality presents no clear demarcation between science and philosophy; and for those few physicists concerned with the foundations of their science, the question of mind becomes more and more important. Many have come to the conclusion that the world beyond appearances is beyond imagination, grasped only through mathematics and such things as quantitative pattern.

Thus, even through physics we could build a strong case that the world of absolute space and time as we experience it with our senses is an illusion. In the Madhyamaka view of Buddhism, just as in physics, when the author here urges us to look at phenomena as dreamlike and to question reality, he assumes that we already have some theoretical foundation for the enquiry. If we introduce this practice into daily life, as we are out walking, for instance, or speaking with other people, we should not be brainwashing ourselves with woolly notions of a dreamlike world. Rather, we should be working from an understanding that phenomena do not exist in the manner in which they appear—an understanding of the theory of Madhyamaka that is beyond the scope of this text, but can be summarized in the ways in which phenomena do exist as dependently related events:

1. Any phenomenon that we identify—a tree, an electron, a galaxy, a person, *any* apprehended object—depends for its existence on our mental designation of it. Without such designation the phenomenon would not exist.
2. All phenomena that participate in natural laws, affecting other entities and themselves arising as effects, depend for their existence on the causal conditions that gave rise to them. For example, the sprout is dependent upon the

seed, the moisture, and the warmth that gave rise to it.

3. For any entity we can identify certain attributes: its component parts, facets, or qualities. The entity depends for its existence on these attributes and would not exist apart from them. At the same time it is neither equivalent to any of these attributes individually, nor to their sum total, nor does it truly exist apart from those attributes.

Thus, phenomena exist as dependently related events, but they do not appear that way. When I look at the mountain across the valley, do I see that its existence depends on its attributes? Do I perceive that the existence of this mountain depends on the mental designation of it, and depends also on its own causes and conditions? I have to say no. The mountain appears to exist entirely in its own right, resting there, utterly self-sufficient. And that is an illusion. In that sense the mountain does not exist as it appears, and in that sense the mountain is dreamlike. This is true of all the environment, and also of our bodies.

Investigate the nature of unborn awareness.

Still exploring the ultimate nature of reality, the author turns in the next verse from the objective world to the investigation of awareness itself. Reflecting philosophically, it quickly becomes apparent that our bodies are not identical to our selves. When we seek something to grasp as our personal identity, we naturally arrive at the mind. What Sechibuwa challenges here is precisely this instinctive sense of personal identity that regards the mind as an entity in its own right. He asks us to investigate whether awareness does in fact exist in its own right, whether our minds exist intrinsically, independent of other people's minds, of the environment, and of our bodies.

Awareness is a more accurate translation than *mind* for the Tibetan word *rigpa* used here. *Mind* is an umbrella term that covers a wide variety of mental events: feelings, memories, imagination, perceptions, intuition, inference. Instead of identifying with this abstract mind that seems to stand apart from all these mental functions even as it directs them, let us focus on the more primitive phenomenon of awareness: simply the sheer presence of consciousness arising from moment to moment. Awareness is the event itself and we can observe it as it arises, not separate from, but in conjunction with, the flavor of each moment: awareness arising with perception, with imagination, with fear, love, anger, recollection, intelligence, or stupidity.

Examine the nature of this awareness, keeping in mind that the goal is to determine whether or not awareness exists intrinsically by its own inherent nature. We can ask first of all, does the awareness we experience exist in the past? No, because the past has ceased. Does it exist in the future? No, because it has not yet arisen. The only awareness we experience is in the present, if in fact it truly exists at all.

And now we can ask a very subtle question. Does our experience of awareness in the present have duration? If our present awareness has no duration at all, we come to a problem. If the present moment of awareness has no duration, then the past also has no duration, being made up of present moments that are completed, and likewise for the future which has not yet begun. And so we would have no duration anywhere.

Let's suppose instead that the experiential moment of present awareness does have duration. It is probably very short, certainly less than a second, because by the end of a second we can already remember its beginning. For the sake of argument, suppose that it lasts one hundredth of a second.

Consider the relationship of this present moment of awareness to its parts. If this awareness has duration, then it must have a beginning, middle, and end; a hundredth of a second can be further divided into thousandths and millionths. The beginning of the present moment cannot be simultaneous with its end, or else it would have no duration. Is this present moment of awareness identical with its own beginning? If so, it would be contained within that beginning and would also have no duration. Is it identical with its end? For the same reason, it cannot be. Nor is it identical with the middle part, because that would leave out the beginning and the end.

If the present moment of awareness is not identical with any one of its parts, is it then identical with all of them—its beginning, middle, and end? This is impossible because these are mutually exclusive sub-moments occurring at different times. No single thing can be identical with other elements that are mutually exclusive. For example, just as a single piece of fruit cannot be both an apple and an orange, so a single moment of awareness cannot be both its beginning and its end. Moreover, this moment also cannot exist apart from its beginning, middle, and end. This is not something that is easily grasped; it is extremely subtle, but worth considering.

This present moment of awareness also has no material form or location. Where is your present moment of awareness of a party you went to when you were a teenager, or of buying your first car, or of making dinner last night? Where is your present moment of awareness of what you are now seeing visually? To locate this is an artificial designation of place. That parts of the brain are associated with these mental events is beyond question, but there are no sound logical or empirical grounds for equating the neurophysiological events with the corresponding experiential, non-physical, non-spatial, formless mental events.

Conventionally speaking, the present moment of awareness arises from the preceding moment of awareness. This continuity of awareness is what enables us to remember the past and also to experience the results of our present mental states in the future, whether in this or later lifetimes. But the previous continuum of awareness is not the only cause of this present moment of awareness. Looking at our experience of these moments as they arise, we can see that the awareness is always referential, relating to something. If we ask, "Awareness of what?" there is always an answer: Awareness of some visual pattern, of sound, of feeling, of recollection, of imagination, of insight, of love, of anger. Awareness exists in an ever-changing causal matrix, modified from moment to moment by internal neurophysiological events, by external physical events, and by other mental events.

Each moment of awareness thus exists as a dependently related event. It is not a "thing"—not a real entity existing in its own right—but an event that occurs in dependence upon other events, inner and outer, that are in a continual state of flux. In the continuum of such mental events we then discover behavioral, cognitive, and emotional patterns. Out of these patterns we develop a sense of personality, which we identify as "I am."

But to equate ourselves with these patterns is fallacious. There is no real personal identity, no "I," no self, in these ever-changing, dependently related events that constitute our stream of awareness. In an ultimate sense, the nature of awareness is unborn; that is, it does not intrinsically arise from some preceding cause. Only on a relative or conventional level can we speak of awareness arising and passing again and again. The concept of mind as an abiding, isolated, changeless entity that performs a variety of mental events—choices, memories, imagination, hopes, fears—that mind as an entity existing in its own right is in fact a non-entity. It is a purely artificial fabrication, and by identifying with that false concept of mind we do ourselves great damage.

At this point the author has discussed both the objective world and subjective awareness, and has concluded that neither exists intrinsically. Whereas he seemed at first to lead us towards idealism, denying that the objective world has any intrinsic reality independent of awareness, he then turns around to deny the intrinsic reality of awareness as well. Both the objective world and the subjective world *do* exist. Their ontological status is fundamentally the same: both exist as matrices of mutually interdependent events, but in neither do we find an absolute foundation for reality. This is neither materialism nor idealism, but something different. How different, we are about to see.

Even the antidote itself is liberated in its own place.

The next verse of the root text continues on the subject of ultimate bodhicitta, or realizing the nature of reality, as a practice during meditation sessions. The direct realization of ultimate truth is the fundamental antidote and ultimate healer of the distortions that afflict the mind. The author is saying that even this realization itself is "liberated in its own place." And here "liberated" means lacking intrinsic existence. Even the realization of ultimate truth is itself devoid of inherent existence.

Sechibuwa has shifted here to a third aspect of reality. After denying first the intrinsic existence of objective reality, and then that of subjective awareness, he now moves on to transcendent awareness. Even this transcendent experience of ultimate reality, in which there is no sense of subject/object, no duality of this as opposed to that, self as opposed to other, no sense of time, no conceptual discrimination—even this fundamental antidote to the fundamental distortion of ignorance has no inherent existence. On what grounds can one make such a statement? The Madhyamaka view proposes the thesis that any dependently related event is devoid of intrinsic existence. Conversely, any entity that is devoid of intrinsic existence is by that very fact a dependently related event. This sums up the ultimate and conventional natures of all phenomena.

Consider whether the non-dual awareness of ultimate truth is a dependently related event. Does it arise in dependence on causes? Experience tells us causes and circumstances do give rise to this non-conceptual realization of emptiness. It results from meditating, cultivating an ethical way of life, developing mental stability and clarity, making intelligent inquiry into the nature of reality, gaining insight, and then repeatedly entering into that awareness. If one lives an immoral life or takes no interest then this realization will not arise. Such awareness therefore does not exist self-sufficiently and absolutely, but depends upon favorable causes and conditions.

This raises a broader issue which is very important in the Madhyamaka view, this most subtle of all Buddhist philoso-

phy. As a hypothetical case, if something were to exist intrinsically, absolutely, and self-sufficiently, what would that imply? What kind of attributes would it necessitate? Nāgārjuna
and other great meditators of the past, following the Buddha
himself, have stated that such an entity would be absolutely
immutable. It would be devoid of change and immune to any
interaction with phenomena other than itself, because any kind
of interaction implies change. It would be utterly and absolutely isolated from anything that is not itself. Moreover, it
would be beyond the scope of awareness, because we know
something only by our consciousness interacting with that object. If, for example, non-dual awareness of ultimate reality
were to exist intrinsically, it would be forever unknowable. The
relationship of this hypothetical entity to its attributes, the
whole to its parts, is also problematic. The investigation of this
problem is another critical avenue leading to the recognition
that phenomena ultimately have no absolute or intrinsic nature.

This leads us to the related topic of the "evolving" Buddha
nature. This awareness, present in every sentient being, is the
continuity that links one lifetime to another, human or otherwise. For most of us it is latent, so obscured by the clutter
on the surface of our minds that we are not aware of its presence. Rather we are aware of the much more superficial conceptualizations, emotions, hopes, fears, anxieties, desires, and
so forth, that shroud the underlying Buddha nature. It is this
Buddha nature which gradually develops into one's awareness
of the full awakening of Buddhahood.

Might this evolving Buddha nature, this innate capacity for
awakening that each of us is endowed with, be intimately associated with the realization of ultimate reality? Certainly there
is a relationship. Does this Buddha nature exist intrinsically?
Is it not independent of any specific life form? We have already said that this continuity does not depend on the specific
form of a given lifetime. But we have to say, once again: No,
even the evolving Buddha nature, which is innate in all of us,
does not exist intrinsically. It too exists as a dependently related
event. In short, there is no conceivable entity—whether ob-

jective, subjective, or non-dual—that has intrinsic existence.

How have we arrived at this conclusion? It is not through blind faith or the simple acceptance of dogma. The only way to arrive at it authentically, with full benefit of the process, is by investigating with integrity, questioning, and applying our full critical awareness and experience. As we bring to mind the hypothetical or assumed intrinsic existence of any phenomenon, the practice eventually leads us to the clarity and certainty that none of these things that have been posited exist intrinsically.

Establish the nature of the path in the sphere of the foundation of all.

Once we have arrived at this point honestly, with insight and intelligence, the nature of the meditative practice shifts. Now we free the mind of the conceptualizations we were using before, free it of any kind of ideation or discursive thought, any conceptual grasping to past, present, or future. The mind relaxes in the nature of non-grasping, and yet we maintain a state of vivid clarity, free of dullness or agitation.

This state is what Chekawa identifies in this next verse. The nature of the path is our own mind and the foundation of all is śūnyatā, or emptiness. The ontological foundation (or absence thereof) of all phenomena is emptiness of inherent existence; and from emptiness arise myriad phenomena, whether objective, subjective, or transcendent. Having arrived at the awareness of that emptiness, you then abide in it free of conceptualization, with the mind at rest, without tension but with vivid clarity.

When conceptualization eventually starts to creep back in, the author advises us at that very moment to direct our awareness to awareness itself. Look right at the conceptualization, and, as it vanishes, maintain the awareness, once again bringing to mind the experience of emptiness. Abide there, he says, relaxing in the sphere of reality, and thereby liberate your mind.

He also encourages us to limit this phase of the meditation

to relatively brief periods. This avoids that spaced-out, non-conceptual state we have all experienced, where the mind is peaceful but not very clear, with no real vividness or insight. We may also return to the more analytical, investigative meditation, arrive once again at the insight, and then again enter the non-conceptual, non-grasping state of awareness. During one sitting we may have numerous short periods of this meditative equipoise.

It's time to ask *why* we should do any of the preceding. Even if the world is illusory in nature, even if objective, subjective, and transcendent phenomena do not exist intrinsically, why should we do any of this? In other words, what's in it for us? The answer is the solution to a fundamental problem.

Our minds are not a blank slate without ideas and assumptions regarding reality, our own existence, the nature of our minds and our environment. On the contrary, we instinctively sense that phenomena, internal and external, exist in their own right. And this causes problems. For example, let us bring to mind someone we really despise. Now see if our mind isn't grasping that person as an entity in his or her own right, intrinsically existent, totally independent, and ultimately responsible for his or her own actions. See if we don't also do the same thing for ourselves. In response to the question, "Who am I?" there naturally arises a sense of "I am," a sense of identification with something that apparently exists intrinsically.

In other words, we are not merely ignorant of the nature of reality but actively, day by day and moment by moment, we are misconstruing the nature of reality. We see things as isolated and intrinsically existing. We reify our own existence and that of friends, loved ones, indifferent people, enemies, the environment itself. And here is the real crux of the matter: this reification is fundamentally out of accord with reality. It creates distortions in the mind and enhances the obscurations that shroud the Buddha nature. In practical terms, it is because of this grasping onto intrinsic reality that a false sense of self arises, as well as the myriad mental distortions that are invariably based on this reification. Jealousy, hatred, resentment, anger, craving, pride, conceit, fear, anxiety—all of these afflictions are based on a misconstruing of reality.

Such reification is the fundamental affliction of the mind; and the realization of emptiness cultivated through this practice acts as an antidote to the fundamental misconstruing of reality. It heals the mind by bringing it into accord with reality. In so doing it attenuates the mental afflictions that are based on that dynamic ignorance until finally they vanish as the Buddha nature is unveiled. In other words, here lies the path to freedom: freedom from suffering, and from the evil, unwholesome actions that arise from mental afflictions. That is the reason for the practice, and it is a pretty good one.

We are coming now to the end of the meditative practice for cultivating the realization of ultimate truth. Sechibuwa instructs us at the end to set aside the subject of meditation. Then, assuming we really believe that this practice is an authentic means for realizing ultimate truth and not just speculative philosophy, he encourages us to cultivate great compassion for those who lack such realization. Whether they are white-collar or blue-collar workers, scientists or religious believers, many of even the most educated and intelligent people grasp unquestioningly onto the intrinsic existence of themselves and other phenomena. And in so doing they cultivate the bed of mental afflictions, from which grow unwholesome actions and the suffering that ensues.

So Sechibuwa suggests that we meditate on great compassion for those who lack such realization. Dedicate this practice to them, with the hope that we may lead them skillfully to deeper and deeper truth, healing them of mental afflictions. Finally, he suggests that we relax if we have been sitting cross-legged or in full lotus position, and he encourages us to end with a devotional practice such as the Seven-Limb Devotion.[1] A devotional practice is very appropriate for the conclusion

---

[1]See my *Tibetan Buddhism from the Ground Up*, forthcoming from Wisdom Publications.

of a meditative practice, wonderfully merging compassion with wisdom.

In studying science or philosophy at a Western university, we are encouraged simply to apply our intellect to solving problems. Great emphasis is laid on reason, encountering paradoxes and solving them, and increasing our intellectual insight. But the study is devoid of a spiritual context, without devotion or reverence. It bears no ostensible relationship to spiritual awakening. On the other hand, in many of the world's religions we find great emphasis on devotion, prayer, humility, and the cultivation of loving kindness. But there is often an absence of any analytical investigation into the nature of reality, the mind, or transcendent experience. All too often we find religious people disparaging reason and delighting in unnecessary paradoxes in the name of Revelation.

Instead, we see here something that merges the two. We can begin with devotions and prayers, asking the ultimate being—as Mañjuśrī or in any other form—to bless us with understanding that is vivid and deep. Bless us that through our investigation into the nature of reality our minds may be healed and we may lead others out of suffering. We then engage in the meditative practice and at the end once again cultivate great compassion, dedicating to others the merit of our investigation. And finally, more devotional practices complete this sublime marriage of wisdom and compassion.

Again I emphasize that we should not accept these practices like a baby swallowing pablum, simply because the verses are written as scripture. The Buddha himself is recorded as encouraging his followers to accept his teachings not out of faith in him, but to test them, as a goldsmith would test gold that he is considering for purchase. Test these teachings in every way possible, because they are not cheap.

If a goldsmith must pay dearly for a piece of metal, he wants to be convinced that he is getting pure gold. Likewise, if we are investing something as precious as our own lives, we want to be very sure that we are investing wisely. And it is our lives that we are investing. Even if our formal practice is limited to an hour or two each day, hopefully we are weaving our spiritual practice into the whole fabric of our waking day so that there is no dichotomy between our work-a-day lives and our spiritual lives. Further, because we are following one type of practice, we are not following myriad others. If we are buying this piece of metal, we are not buying all the metal that is being sold by others.

For this reason, any qualms we might have concerning this practice are to be acknowledged, bringing them front and center, even writing them down. We may pick up other books on the topic to see if we can dispel some of our doubts on our own. Once we feel that we have clarified an uncertainty, we can check with an experienced teacher whether our insight is in fact accurate, or whether it is slightly or even totally off the mark. Frequently the most effective way to confront and work through uncertainties is to discuss them with someone who is well grounded in both the theoretical and practical aspects of the teachings. Discuss them with an open mind and without fear, not feeling that we have to contort our views into some established pattern. A deep faith in Buddhadharma expresses itself as an intelligent faith.

Between meditation sessions act as an illusory being.

Following the meditative practice for gaining realization of ultimate truth, Sechibuwa discusses a post-meditative practice for enhancing the realization. What is an illusory being? An illusion is something that appears in a manner in which it does not exist. A common analogy in Buddhist writings is that of an Indian magician creating an illusion of horses and elephants. The spectators looking at the illusion actually see horses and elephants, seemingly every bit as real as if they really existed. The mode of appearance conflicts with the mode of existence, suggesting something far more substantial than the actual reality. To counteract that mental distortion, the author encourages us between sessions to act with the awareness that the self is like an illusion. Recognize that while we perceive our personal identity as a substantial self, in fact there is no such "I" as an intrinsic, inherently existent self. Rather, we exist as dependently related events.

What does this mean in actual practice? Imagine that you have entered into the analytical meditation on emptiness, where you examine with full clarity of mind whether phenomena, including awareness, exist intrinsically or whether they are in fact empty of intrinsic existence, and thus appear like a dream or illusion. You then go from the analytical meditation into the space-like meditation, leaving behind any conceptualization of subject and object and abiding in this non-dual awareness. Having done that, you feel that your meditation session is about to end. You arise from it, but you seek to maintain that sense of the lack of intrinsic existence of the phenomena around you, of your own awareness, and of your self.

Arise from the meditation cushion maintaining a continuity between the insight that you had during the meditation and your mental state afterwards. As you stand up, walk to the door, or speak to someone, try to maintain the awareness that phenomena—including your self, your mind, other people you come in contact with, everything around you—exist not as intrinsic entities, but as dependently related events.

The profound, innate interdependence of phenomena is not normally apparent to us. We must go beyond appearances and introduce insight. For example, how do I exist as a dependently related event? In Buddhism we speak of the five *skandhas*, or psychophysical aggregates: the body, feelings, discrimination, mental events (such as thoughts, imagination, recollection, and volition) and finally consciousness itself, whether sensory or mental. All of these exist as dependently related events; none exists as an independent entity. And in none of these can we find an "I," a self, an intrinsic "myness." My self conventionally exists in the flux of these five psychophysical aggregates, in dependence upon them. I exist, not among them, not apart from them, but mentally designated upon them.

This means that if I seek my self among my physical or mental constituents, I am nowhere to be found—neither among them, nor as their sum total, nor apart from them. Why is this? Because I exist as a dependently related event. Dependent upon what? I exist in dependence upon my mental designation of my self. I conceive of myself and in so doing I mentally designate myself on the basis of things that are not myself.

A very practical way to integrate the meditative practice with the post-meditative practice is to refresh this awareness, again and again, of how phenomena are dependent for their very existence upon mental designation. Take the example of a cart. None of its parts is the cart itself. No one thing can simultaneously be the axle *and* the wheel *and* the flat bottom. These are totally different entities with their own defining qualities such as flatness or roundness. The cart is not the wheel, nor is it the flat bottom, nor the axle. Nor is it all of the above, because one thing cannot be all of the mutually exclusive parts of the cart. The cart is not identical with any one of its parts, nor is it equivalent to the sum of the parts. But if you take away each of the parts, then there is no cart remaining. What is a cart? It is something that is mentally designated upon the parts. Does the cart that is so designated perform the function of a cart? Yes: it carries hay and people; it travels; it is pulled by horses.

Likewise, I perform the functions of a person. I speak, I think, I act. Yet I am not the speech, the thought, or the deed. I am not the body or the mind. I am designated upon the body and mind, and my self depends for its very existence upon this mental designation. Like all phenomena, both subjective and objective, my self does not exist in its own right.

In other words, no object exists from its own side exclusively, presenting all of its own characteristics by itself. Rather, in the act of identifying things we are co-producers of the objects we perceive. How does this occur? In what way are we co-producers of the events that present themselves to us? As we reach out with the mind in response to events, we identify them—as joy, ill health, poverty, wealth, and so forth. We conceptually designate them and we thereby create the world we experience, moment by moment. Keep in mind that these events are also created as a result of our own actions in previous lives, or possibly as the fruit of especially potent actions performed earlier in this very life. We are finally responsible for the events that we encounter.

If we were to leave it at that, the universe would be a deterministic machine. Where is the potential for creativity, for implementing wisdom and compassion? The field of Dharma as a spiritual practice lies in how we respond to the events that we encounter, be they pleasant, unpleasant or indifferent. How do we respond? Predictably, in a life devoid of Dharma the response to misfortune is anger, resentment, and fear. When prosperity arises, the response is attachment, clinging, and anxiety in anticipation of loss. When events are neither pleasing nor unpleasing, the response is indifference; the mind is cloudy and sluggish in ignorance. In this mechanical behavior we recognize the three poisons: anger, craving, and confusion.

In Dharma, the creativity of spiritual practice lies in transforming our responses to the myriad events that present themselves to us. A profound aspect of this practice is to recognize how we have created, and are still creating, the events, objects, and people we encounter by the manner in which we mentally identify them. Our daily spiritual practice is profoundly empowered when we bring to it this insight into the emptiness of intrinsic identity of phenomena.

Even in something as simple as offering a glass of water, we may be aware that "I," the giver, am not intrinsically existent. The giver exists in dependence upon the process of giving. Likewise, the gift, the recipient, and the giving itself also do not exist intrinsically. There can be no giving without a recipient, and there is no such thing as a gift without the giver and the recipient. All three, giver, gift, and recipient, are mutually interdependent. Each exists as a dependently related event and none exists intrinsically. If we bring this awareness into the act, offering a glass of water becomes a powerfully transforming spiritual practice.

You can see how the meditative practice that enhances our

realization also deepens our experience between sessions; and this in turn still further deepens our meditative experience. The two are complementary, enhancing one another.

THE CULTIVATION OF RELATIVE BODHICITTA

Following the discussion of ultimate bodhicitta, the second point of the Seven-Point Mind Training continues with the cultivation of relative bodhicitta, specifically through the practice known as exchanging self for others. It is a very powerful practice, central to the spirit of awakening, and also very similar to Christian practice.

Sechibuwa begins his explanation with a quote from Śāntideva, the great Indian bodhisattva: "One who wishes swiftly to protect oneself and others should engage in the secret and holy practice of exchanging self for others."[2] If we fail to exchange our happiness for the suffering of others, we will not become fully awakened, nor will there be any joy in the cycle of existence. If we wish to subdue the harm that comes our way, and also pacify the sufferings of others, we should offer ourselves to others and cherish others as ourselves.

Just as in the cultivation of ultimate bodhicitta, the author deals first with the practice during meditation before introducing other practices for post-meditation periods.

Alternately practice sending and taking.

To understand what this next verse of the root text means, let's simply follow Sechibuwa's commentary. He suggests that we sit comfortably on a cushion and while clearly visualizing our mother, cultivate loving kindness and compassion for her.

It seems crucial, and profoundly beneficial, that he chooses to begin with our own mother. If we do not have a loving relationship with our own parents, something is going to be awry

---

[2]*Bodhisattvacaryāvatāra*, VIII, 120. All translations are mine unless otherwise indicated.

at the very core of our spiritual practice, creating disharmony throughout our lives. I say this not naively, but knowing that some parents abuse their children sexually, physically, or psychologically. Marriages break up, leaving children with confused feelings toward their parents. Those of us with ill-feeling towards a mother or father may be tempted to say: "This is hard for me because I had a rotten childhood. I'll skip my parents and begin instead on firmer ground, with a close friend, or my wife or husband."

There is, of course, no law against this. But as long as our feelings remain unresolved towards our own parents, we lack a firm foundation for other relationships. Regardless of how our parents have treated us, it is crucial for a balanced and harmonious life that we come to terms with any resentment that we feel, and so bring insight to bear on the relationship that loving kindness and compassion can arise from the heart. By beginning with our mother, we establish a root from which to let this compassion flow out to our father, to other relatives and friends, to people about whom we feel indifferent, and finally to our enemies.

Sechibuwa encourages us first to reflect that our mother has given us this precious, fully endowed human life, which means, in essence, that we have time for spiritual practice if we do no more than shift our priorities. In this lifetime, for the most part, many of us have good health, sufficient food, clothing, lodging, and education. We are intelligent, our faculties intact. We have encountered spiritual guidance indirectly from a fully awakened being, the Buddha, and we have met with competent spiritual guides here in this lifetime. Moreover, we wish to heal our minds, to bring greater meaning into our lives, and to follow the path of awakening.

How did these opportunities arise? Because of our mother. Regardless of how she might have treated us afterwards, it is because she gave us birth that we have a wonderful potential for spiritual growth in this and future lives. Our mother opened the door for these present opportunities. And many of us have had very good mothers who cared for us with love and affection, raised us not to squander our lives, and enabled us to encounter the teachings of a fully awakened being.

Consider how a mother responds to her child. Those who are mothers or fathers themselves will see this especially clearly. The concern begins even before birth while she carries her child for nine months; the event of the birth; the great effort—sometimes joyful, sometimes less so—of raising the infant through thousands of diaper changes and feedings; teaching the child to walk, to speak, to relate to other children; responding to illness; providing for schooling; continuing to look after the child's welfare, on and on, through puberty and early adulthood. Parents never stop being parents to their children. What a tremendous investment of effort and time and, in most cases, a tremendous expression of love, concern, and affection! Each of us has received this, in varying degrees, from our own mother.

Those of us who believe in the sequence of life after life can look to the past while focusing on our present mother. We can meditate on the kindness our mother has shown us not only in this life but also in previous lives, because surely this is not the first time we have known this person. Such an intimate relationship almost certainly arises as a result of a very close relationship in a previous life. It is even possible, though not certain, that our mother was also our mother in the last life. But that she has been our mother in previous lives, we can be sure. And so from life to life, our mother has cherished and cared for us in an ongoing relationship.

This meditation of simply reflecting upon the kindness, care, and affection that our mother has shown us is very important, regardless of the deepest benefits that may fully ripen only in future lives. As we reflect deeply, and really feel in our hearts the great compassion and kindness shown to us by our mother, this naturally gives rise to a yearning to repay the kindness: "How can I serve her now, as she ages, as her health begins to fail, as she approaches death? How can I help her in return? I would like to give her every joy and happiness, and protect her from all harm."

Think too, says Sechibuwa, that while our mother has cared for us so long in this and previous lifetimes, sometimes even sacrificing her life for her children, she has meanwhile suffered grief, anxiety, fear, and physical pain. Not only because of her children, but throughout the course of her life, she has experienced the suffering of mental afflictions, aging, sickness, and death. As we ponder this, a feeling of compassion for our mother arises without much effort. Compassion, in this case, is simply the wish, "May you be free of suffering."

Take the example of a mother who is a drunkard. We can reflect upon the unhappiness, the lack of satisfaction and meaning in life that gave rise to a habit of drinking and made her dependent on alcohol to get through each day. If a mother is an alcoholic, it naturally follows that sometimes she is not a very conscientious mother; and thirty or forty years later the child may still suffer resentment. But as we feel compassion for her, we can empathize with the sorrow and anxiety that gave rise to the affliction of alcohol dependency. And we can wish from our hearts, sincerely and without hypocrisy, "May you be free both from the dependency, and from the unsatisfied need that gave rise to it. May you be free of the suffering as well as its inner source."

Imagine now the suffering that your own mother experiences. For this potent practice to be done correctly, it must become a very personal meditation on your own mother. Bring to mind the suffering you have seen her experience, physical or mental, related to her internal condition or external circumstances. Go right to the source of the suffering, the basic mental afflictions themselves: attachment, hostility, ignorance. Imagine her own experience of the suffering, particularly if you have a mother who is handicapped by a problem such as drinking.

Practice "taking" this suffering. Imagine taking upon yourself your own mother's suffering together with its sources: all the mental distortions and the instincts for their arising. Imagine that you are peeling this off her, removing it from her continuum. As Sechibuwa says, "Slice it off with a knife." Imagine it as dense, black smoke; draw this black smoke from her and bring it into your heart. Visualize a blackness there in your own heart, like a black egg or sphere, symbolizing your own self-centeredness. Draw in the black smoke of suffering and its sources, and dissolve it into this blackness at your own heart. The point here is not to imagine yourself experiencing your mother's anger, pain, or confusion. Instead, imagine that the suffering comes directly into your heart, specifically to the self-centeredness in your heart, and totally annihilates it, leaving not a single trace.

As you draw in the black smoke, see your mother in your mind's eye arising from the suffering and the mental afflictions that are its source. For example, if she suffers from arthritis, imagine her looking at her hands and her joints, moving them freely and delighting in the experience of the full and proper use of her limbs, her back, her neck. Imagine her regaining vibrant health. If strife or anger plague her, imagine the anger quelled, the strife pacified. Imagine her serene, content, at peace with her surroundings. If she is anxious by nature, see her face becoming calm, relaxing as you draw out the black smoke of her worries.

In this way, imagine taking off layer after layer of internal and external unhappiness and misfortune, and dissolving them into your own heart. This is the practice of "taking" as applied to our mother, the first half of the practice for the cultivation of relative bodhicitta.

The second half of the practice is known as "sending" or "giving." Let the aspiration arise: "May I bring about all happiness for my own mother." Imagine that you are giving your body, your possessions, and all your virtue, without any sense of reservation, to your mother. Imagine sending this in the form of a white light that radiates from a precious jewel at your heart, a jewel from which all favorable circumstances for your mother come forth: food, clothing, dwelling, helpers, and spiritual guidance. Imagine her being endowed with everything she needs for the realization of full awakening.

Once again, let the full wealth of your imagination be brought to bear in this practice. Visualize this jewel fulfilling her wishes,

so that she can put them aside. If we really long for something worldly, it may well enhance our spiritual practice to
satisfy that mundane desire and thus dispense with it. Imagine
her desires fulfilled so they no longer nag at her mind. Contented, she recognizes this as insufficient and longs for full
awakening.

Imagine her meeting with all favorable circumstances for her
spiritual growth, the purification of her mind, and cultivation
of wholesome qualities. Imagine it as clearly as you can. Imagine her growing in this way, maturing along her own spiritual
path. If your mother is a Christian, imagine her meeting with
a very fine Christian mentor, her devotion deepening, and her
life more and more emulating that of Jesus Christ. Imagine
her receiving the fullest possible benefit from this spiritual path
and following it more and more deeply. Imagine her attaining
full awakening. Imagine the qualities that would arise; how
her personality would be transformed. Imagine the loving kindness, the wisdom, the ability for serving others that would arise,
and then, finally, imagine her attaining full awakening.

Gain some familiarity with both taking and sending in this
practice. As you become familiar with them separately, practice them alternately, first taking and then sending. Let them
enhance and enrich one another. At times go back and simply allow the affection for your mother to arise with a heart-
felt concern for her well-being. Then once again, on the basis
of loving kindness and compassion, practice taking and sending. Sechibuwa writes: "Truly long to be able to give her all
happiness, even offering her your body, your own possessions,
your own virtues."

Virtue in this context means the wholesome imprints on your
mind stream. Keep in mind that this is the very source of your
future happiness, what brings you success in mundane as well
as in spiritual matters. Imagine offering this up to her as well.

In Buddhism there is a lot of talk about virtue, or merit,
that is accumulated by service, meditation, or study. It is possible to become avaricious about this merit. We may weigh
our actions for their potential merit, or choose to make this

offering rather than that one because of the relative merit. Merit is a reality, and it plays a very crucial role in spiritual practice, but we should not become merit-misers. The antidote is to be aware that, because there is such a thing as merit, it can be offered. Does this mean that if you deeply desire to offer up all of your merit to your mother, it will in fact be moved from your account to your mother's ledger, leaving you with nothing at all? In fact this is not possible, but by offering to others our own merits, we enhance and compound these virtuous imprints.

Having understood this, we should not dwell on it. The point of the practice is to release the attachment we have to our own body, possessions, and virtues—not only to detach ourselves from them, but also to offer them sincerely for the service of others. So we start with our mother to experience the longing, "If I only could offer you my merit, my body, my possessions."

To some extent of course we can. If our mother is in need and we can in fact help her, then the meditation must manifest in external activity and not remain on the level of imagination. Let the compassion that arises be not simply an armchair compassion, such that we sit here and think these very nice thoughts and then treat her thoughtlessly or repeat old, unwholesome patterns. Rather, let the meditation while we are in solitude arise into our aspirations and, as in the previous meditation on ultimate bodhicitta, let it then be integrated in our actions following meditation so that we really develop the intention to serve our mother.

This practice of taking and sending with regard to our mother can constitute the first session of meditation. We might want to take a break before expanding this practice in a second session to focus on other people: our father, for example, or close friends. Then gradually move on to indifferent people and finally to those whom we really dislike.

In each case, it is very helpful to meditate first on the kindness of these other beings. Meditating on our friends' good qualities is an easy beginning. Then take one friend to mind and think of this person's misfortunes and the specific kinds of suffering to which he or she is subject. Place yourself in this person's shoes and imagine experiencing her anxieties. Then begin the practice of taking: take into your heart as a black smoke the mental and physical suffering of this person, as well as the mental distortions that give rise to such suffering.

Repeat this with one, two, ten, or twenty different people, from session to session, day to day, until the practice becomes very fluent. Gradually include people whom you regard with indifference. Here the practice becomes extremely potent. Focus again and again on such people, recognizing that just like us they wish to experience happiness and be free of suffering. This is the bottom line. Regardless of whatever kindness they may or may not have rendered to us in any observable way, we are kin. We belong to the same family of sentient beings.

The practice is the same in each case: taking suffering, taking the sources of suffering, then offering your body, your possessions, and your merits. Just as you did with your mother, send them all causes and favorable circumstances for their spiritual growth, so that they can recognize the inner source of their discontent and not mistake it for some external situation. Send them the circumstances that will enable them to follow the path of their choice, purifying their minds of the sources of misery, confusion, and strife, and bringing them to joy that arises from the essential nature of the mind itself, rather than from some pleasant stimulus.

We are working up to the enemy. Don't postpone this facet of the practice, thinking you are not ready; it is worth entering soon. Plunge in and bring to mind a person you really cannot stand. Perhaps someone has treated you contemptuously, abused you, or taken something that you really cherished. For whatever reason, repugnance may arise toward a certain person. Perhaps they have really done nothing wrong at all, but something about their personality or behavior gives rise to abhorrence.

Because it is a mental distortion, hostility towards another person tends to be fundamentally stupid. As we look at a person with objectionable qualities, hatred invariably grasps onto that person as existing intrinsically. Because hatred itself derives from the ignorance of grasping onto such intrinsic existence, it naturally carries that same characteristic of ignorance with it. Hostility is stupid in the sense that it ignores the manifold causes and conditions that have given rise over years and years, lifetime after lifetime, to the present characteristics of the person in question.

To some extent we may be free of the qualities that we find so abhorrent in another person, especially if we have had the benefit of excellent teachers and a background in Dharma. Has the other person been so fortunate? Has that person had close and meaningful contact with authentic spiritual guides who can show them the source of their suffering? Or have they been deprived of this precious guidance?

Anger tends to ignore a person's history, to reify him, and hold him intrinsically, autonomously responsible for every objectionable quality. Anger does something else: it hones in on small instances in which this person seemed especially obnoxious, narrow-minded, or superficial. On the basis of selected vignettes, perhaps even without direct contact, we build a caricature. In the mind of our own anger, we build a conceptual construct of a human being who has only negative qualities, a person with no Buddha nature. We look at this cartoon of our own creation that has no existence at all as a human being, because no human being can exist totally saturated to the core with repugnant qualities, and we feel, "How disgusting you are!" Of course what appears in our mind's eye is disgusting and repulsive; it is also a fabrication of our own distorted mind.

Let's come back to the real person. I am not suggesting that every disagreeable quality we perceive in others is a fallacy and that everyone, with the exception of ourselves, is pristine pure. People are three-dimensional. Every single person is endowed with Buddha nature, and every single person has a history. As we seek to cultivate loving kindness and compassion for people we dislike, and on that basis to practice sending and taking, it is invaluable to keep their personal histories in mind. Even if we know nothing about them, we can infer that there have been causes and conditions that gave rise to the behavior we perceive. When our minds are settling in meditation, with hopefully greater clarity than normal, we can seek out in the mind's eye occasions when these people did not display repugnant qualities. Anger does not care about those times at all; it wants to sift them out and completely forget about them. Balance anger's view with the Dharma view, based on intelligent faith, that each of us—enemy, friend, indifferent person, or self—is endowed with Buddha nature. Each of us at our core is utterly pristine and untainted by mental distortions.

Now integrate this with the practice of taking and sending. In the first act of taking, identify the specific disagreeable behavior or personality traits that you find repugnant in this person. More than likely they are mental distortions or direct expressions of them. Here the term "mental afflictions" is very helpful. Anger, attachment, and ignorance are not bad simply because they produce bad results on some future occasion. Even as they arise they hurt, causing some degree of subtle or gross suffering.

Bring these afflictions to mind, and feel compassion for this person who suffers their disease, recognizing that we ourselves are not immune, although the afflictions may be temporarily attenuated. We are not yet free, and we can imagine future circumstances that might prompt similar behavior from ourselves. This is a brother, a sister, we are dealing with. To be subject to such afflictions, and the actions that derive from them, is indeed to suffer as a victim.

Imagine, in empathy and kinship, taking the black smoke into the blackness of self-centeredness at your own heart. Peel the suffering and its source off that person. As you do so, hold the person as clearly as possible in your mind's eye, and imagine him or her free of repugnant qualities and behavior.

Then, in the practice of sending offer your body, possessions, and merit, so that this person's mind may become clearer and his heart warmer and more open, so that he or she might recognize wholesome behavior and delight in cultivating it. Imagine this person becoming a bodhisattva and gaining deeper and deeper insight. Imagine your body as a jewel sending out all favorable circumstances for his or her spiritual maturation. Finally, imagine this person becoming a fully awakened being.

Once we have practiced taking and sending in this manner with regards to mother, father, friends, indifferent people, and finally our enemies, we can take a 360-degree approach, and reach out to every sentient being. Saying "every sentient being" avoids the blurry vastness of "all sentient beings," which can become an impersonal "to whom it may concern." Recognize that this includes the animals, human beings of all races, all worlds, and all other types of sentient beings. As before, practice taking and sending on the basis of loving kindness and compassion for each and every sentient being.

Sechibuwa encourages us to practice this not only in purely mental meditation, but also to recite verses verbally to this effect. For example, express in words the aspiration, "May I become a cause of all worldly and transcendent joy for every sentient being. May I become a cause for dispelling the suffering of every sentient being." There are some very beautiful lines to this effect in the third chapter of Śāntideva's *A Guide to the Bodhisattva's Way of Life.* The idea is to saturate our mind, our voice, and our physical activities in the practice of taking and sending.

Apply those two to the breath.

The next verse of the root text offers a wonderful extension to the practice of taking and sending. It also adds a new dimension to the practice of breath awareness, though it should not replace straight breath awareness as a substitute. This rich but very simple practice has its own fruits.

As you inhale while focusing on your mother or another person, take in the suffering in the form of black smoke. Then, as you exhale, send out white light offering all you have for that person's well-being. With each in-breath, take in and with each out-breath, send out; taking and sending again and again. You can do this in the solitude of meditation, but also very effectively when the suffering of others confronts you directly. When you see someone who is angry or in pain, when you visit someone in the hospital, or watch the news of some calamity, practice right there on the spot. Since you are already breathing, you might as well make it more meaningful.

Three objects, three poisons, three roots of virtue.

The next verse refers to the three objects: agreeable, disagreeable, and neutral objects. As we relate to these three types of objects, the three mental poisons arise: attachment, hostility, and confusion. The point is to use these poisons as opportunities to nurture the roots of virtue.

As we engage in the affairs of daily life, as soon as we become aware that attachment, craving, or clinging has arisen, right then is the time to recognize that there are an immeasurable number of sentient beings who are subject to the same mental afflictions. Expand your awareness of this right on the spot, and let the aspiration arise: "May those countless sentient beings be endowed with the root of virtue that is freedom from attachment. May they be free of this attachment that I am now experiencing." The aspiration itself is a root of virtue.

Similarly, in moments of anger, simply recognize the anger as it arises. This presents a way for those of us with a Dharma friend or spouse to help each other. Provided the anger is not directed at the other person, when one flies off the handle the other can simply say, "Anger has arisen." This can, if not vanquish the anger, at least snap us halfway out of its craziness. The anger presents us also with the opportunity, once we have recognized it, to recognize also that there are innumerable sentient beings who, like ourselves, are subject to anger. And so let the aspiration arise: "May they be endowed with the root of virtue of freedom from anger." We can likewise apply the same practice to the third poison, confusion or ignorance. This is truly a practice for our daily life.

In all activities train with words.

In this final verse of the second point, we are encouraged to recite phrases in accord with the practice of taking and sending, particularly when we are alone. For example, Sechibuwa suggests the words, "May the suffering of all sentient beings be drawn to me." Keep in mind that this means "be drawn to my own self-centeredness, that it may be vanquished." Another example he offers is, "By my joy may all beings experience joy." The point of uttering such words is to saturate the mind and the heart in these thoughts for the cultivation of relative bodhicitta.

The Third Point
Using Unfavorable Circumstances as Aids to Awakening

The use of unfavorable circumstances as aids to spiritual awakening is perhaps the best-known aspect of the Seven-Point Mind Training, and constitutes a very substantial part of the text.

When the environment and its inhabitants are enslaved by evil, transform unfavorable circumstances into the path of awakening.

When Sechibuwa finished his notes on Chekawa's discourses, he commented that the environment of his own day and age really fit the bill: an evil time when unwholesome thoughts and deeds were rampant. He was writing in the twelfth century in Tibet, but his words are equally pertinent to our experience in the twentieth century. He states emphatically that, although there are a vast number of practices within the Buddhadharma—tantric practices, the cultivation of meditative quiescence, meditation on emptiness and many hundreds of others—not one will bear proper fruit in the absence of a mind-training practice and, more specifically, the ability to transform unfavorable circumstances into the path.

I always have been leery of the claim, "This way is the only way; anything else is a waste of time," but I believe that Sechibuwa is perfectly justified in making this statement. This is not to say that Tibetan Buddhism, or the Seven-Point Mind Training, has a monopoly on transforming unfavorable circumstances into the spiritual path. But unless we are skilled in dealing with such circumstances and can digest them into our spiritual practice rather than groaning in complaint or merely praying that they pass, then our chances are extremely remote for stabilizing the mind, developing bodhicitta, or progressing in any kind of tantric practice.

The approach that Sechibuwa recommends first is simply to bear in mind that whatever misfortune we experience comes as a result of our actions in previous lives. In Buddhism, evil or unwholesomeness is defined in terms of its fully ripening effect. The full maturation of a very potent deed may occur later in the same lifetime, though more frequently the full karmic effects of a deed ripen in a future lifetime. If the full maturation consists of misfortune, suffering, or grief, then by definition the deed that gave rise to that result is unwholesome. Thus, Buddhism claims the existence of a natural morality. There are distinctions between wholesome and unwholesome deeds that hold true for all beings, human or otherwise. It is simply in the nature of things that certain actions, even mental actions such as malice, are unwholesome.[1]

When unfavorable circumstances occur, from a serious ill-

---

[1]On another level, ethics are more narrowly delineated for people who have taken precepts. For example, it is unwholesome for an ordained Buddhist monk to cut down trees, or even to cut living vegetables. Regardless of the specific reasons for the prohibition, the deed is unwholesome because of one's commitment to the precept. It is not unwholesome for someone who has not taken this precept to cut down a tree or cut vegetables. Many of the monastic vows relate to the polite customs of India in another day and age, with no clear line of demarcation between common courtesy and ethics. Recognizing that this can change, Buddha made the comment shortly before his death that these and secondary precepts could be altered to keep them relevant in the future.

ness to a simple interruption in meditation, some people may groan helplessly in response to the obstacle. But those who have truly entered the door of Dharma will begin to respond actively to unfavorable circumstances in a way that transforms them. How? By cultivating the attitude that whatever misfortune may arise is a blessing of the spiritual mentor and the Triple Gem of Buddha, Dharma, and Saṃgha. This is not to say that your teacher is throwing you curve balls in an effort to mess up your life, or that the Buddhas are out to get you. Buddhism does not attribute the vicissitudes of life to the whims of an ultimate being.

Instead, bear in mind that this teaching assumes that we have begun to cultivate ultimate bodhicitta, and to understand the lack of intrinsic identity of phenomena. Misfortunes and obstacles to practice do not exist intrinsically. For something to be a misfortune for me, I must identify it as such. If I refuse to identify something as an obstacle but say instead, "I accept this illness as a blessing of my spiritual guide and of the Buddha," then it becomes so. It takes much courage and knowledge of Dharma to say that, to mean it, and to act accordingly, but it is extremely potent. We can then rebound from these calamities with courage and understanding, instead of wilting under their pressure; and this is necessary for a deep and fruitful practice.

In his discussion of transforming unfavorable circumstances into the path of awakening, Sechibuwa addresses two aspects of the practice. One is purely mental and the other is expressed through action. The first of these concerns an adjustment of attitude, and this transformation of the mind is examined in terms of both relative and ultimate bodhicitta.

Beginning with relative bodhicitta, Sechibuwa recommends that we distinguish between enemy and friend. The enemy is self-centeredness: the priority or value judgment that expresses itself in such thoughts as, "My well-being is more important than that of any other individual. I come first. If anyone is to be praised, it should be me. If one thing is better than others, then I should have the best. If one person has to lose and another to win, I should win."

This attitude is the enemy. By definition, an enemy brings us suffering. It may be the mental suffering of abuse, contempt, or slander; or the attack may lead to physical suffering. As we look more closely at self-centeredness, we will see that it fits the definition exactly. But if self-centeredness is the enemy, what is the friend? Concern for the welfare of others. The beauty of this thought lies in the nature of our existence. Given that all of us exist as dependently related events, devoid of any isolated, individual existence, we must move with an awareness of the well-being of others around us. We must open our minds to this infinity, and not only to another individual here and there. Just as our interdependence with the rest of life is not cut off at any point, our concern for others should not be limited arbitrarily. Instead, leave it wide open and boundless. There is no inherent cut-off point between ourselves and life around us, just as there is no inherent cut-off point between America and other continents, between human beings, animals, and other types of sentient beings.

In the Buddhist world view the universe is infinite and there is an infinity of life in the universe. To cultivate this attitude of cherishing others with affection and concern for their welfare is to act in perfect accord with reality, priming ourselves for the realization of emptiness.

Unless we make this distinction between friend and enemy, self-centeredness can motivate all our mundane activities. Cherishing others can become an extension of self-centeredness: "My spouse, my children, my relatives, my friends are all necessary for my well-being, just like my other possessions; and for this reason I care for them." Likewise, self-centeredness may be rampant in our spiritual activities. We may meditate, go to teachings, do retreats, all in order to find greater peace in this lifetime for ourselves. Even if we deepen this by taking future lives into account, we may still be motivated by the avoidance of our own future misery. We may even aspire to attain Buddhahood...for our own well-being. All of these are expressions of self-centeredness.

Sechibuwa emphasizes that any Dharma practice motivated by self-centeredness is faulty. Mahāyāna Buddhist teachings express the view that no spiritual practice, whether the deepest meditation taught in the *sūtras* or the completion stage of Highest Yoga Tantra, can lead to full awakening if motivated by self-centeredness.

Blame everything on one thing.

The next verse instructs us to blame everything bad that happens to us, from tragedy to ingrown toenails, on one thing alone: self-centeredness. This is a very powerful antidote to a very natural tendency. When we experience misfortune, we almost invariably look outward and say, "Who did this to me?" If we identify a perpetrator, myriad mental distortions arise in response. Another person may well have acted as a co-operative condition contributing to our unhappiness, but that person is not the real cause.

On the deepest level, taking karma into account, we are ultimately responsible for our present circumstances, and for the future we are creating right now with each action of body, speech, and mind. But we are responsible on another level also which can be helpful to consider. Imagine, for example, that someone drives into my car and puts a dent in it. In this particular instance I am blameless; my car was stationary. I can target the person who did it, and that person seems truly to blame for my suffering—the dent in my nice new car. But remember how our enemies first appeared when we approached them in the practice of taking and sending. I have isolated this person. It's a sure bet that I am looking at the person who dented my car as an intrinsic, autonomous entity, and in this way I feed the fires of my indignation and self-righteousness.

What is the real issue here? Was I at fault in this particular context? Both the law and my insurance company would say that I was not. Someone has damaged a possession of mine and I have no freedom to choose whether or not I experience this particular circumstance. On a deep level I have stacked the cards to experience this through my own previous actions. But here lies the freedom: How do I respond? The dent in the car has no power to cause me any suffering unless I yield to it. The dent is only an external catalyst, a contributing circumstance, but by itself it is not sufficient to cause me suffering.

What are the added ingredients that cause me suffering? First of all, I had to possess the car. Watching someone drive into another person's car does not have the same impact on me as watching someone drive into mine. At a minimum, the suffering requires a person to drive into the car, the car that was driven into, and my possession of the car. But all this is still insufficient for suffering to arise in my mind. We have the ingredients for a cake but no oven. The suffering actually arises from the stuff of my own mind. If I were mindless there would be no suffering, but that is not an option. I cannot decide to reject my mind. Instead I must apply my intelligence: What element of my mind was responsible for my suffering?

The real source of my suffering is self-centeredness: *my* car, *my* possession, *my* well-being. Without the self-centeredness, the suffering would not arise. What would happen instead? It is important to imagine this fully and to focus on examples of your own. Think of some misfortune that makes you want to lash out, that gives rise to anger or misery. Then imagine how you might respond without suffering. Recognize that we need not experience the misery, let alone the anger, resentment, and hostility. The choice is ours.

Let's continue with the previous example. You see that there is a dent in the car. What needs to be done? Get the other driver's license number, notify the police, contact the insurance agency, deal with all the details. Simply do it and accept it. Accept it gladly as a way to strengthen your mind further, to develop patience and the armor of forbearance. There is no way to become a Buddha and remain a vulnerable wimp. Patience does not suddenly appear as a bonus after full enlightenment. Part of the whole process of awakening is to develop greater forbearance and equanimity in adversity. Śāntideva, in the sixth chapter of his *Guide to the Bodhisattva's Way of Life*, eloquently points out that there is no way to develop patience without encountering adversity, and patience is indispensable for our own growth on the path to awakening.

So think of your own example. Recognize that anger or resentment is superfluous mental garbage, and that clutter and distortion serve no useful purpose in our minds. Suffering is not even necessary. Geshe Ngawang Dhargyey once made the comment that, once bodhicitta has been developed to the point of arising spontaneously, one becomes a bodhisattva and no longer experiences the common sorts of mental suffering. Although a bodhisattva may experience suffering in sympathy for others, the kind of self-oriented suffering we normally experience simply does not happen, because a bodhisattva is free of self-centeredness.

Blame everything on one thing. It simplifies life incredibly, and yet it truly is not simplistic. If we believe from our hearts that all of our misfortunes can be attributed to self-centeredness, this must radically transform our lives.

Do we have reservations? Isn't there some part of the mind that says, "Self-centeredness is not such a bad idea. It got me my job, a good salary, my house and car. How can this be my enemy?" On the surface self-centeredness may seem like an aide who looks after our interests. There is one powerful answer to this: insofar as self-centeredness dominates our lives, it brings us into conflict with virtually everyone else. Because most people are dominated by self-centeredness, their interests are at odds with our own. There is bound to be conflict, and conflict gives rise to suffering.

Imagine what life would be like without self-centeredness. Would we give away all our possessions, waste away from malnutrition, and die prematurely of disease? No. This would be a partial lack of self-centeredness combined with a large part of stupidity. If we are to serve others effectively, we must take care of ourselves. A bodhisattva has no self-centeredness, but there have been people in all stations of life, including kings, who are bodhisattvas. If we free ourselves of self-centeredness and really concern ourselves with the cherishing of others, then our own welfare comes as a kind of echo.

There are an infinite number of ways to serve the well-being of others. The motivation of cherishing others can engage the energies of a doctor, a teacher, a carpenter, or an auto mechanic; or it can move us to withdraw from active service to train for helping others. Any attention to our own welfare comes as a repercussion of this concern for others.

Well-being, contentment, and good cheer come also as side-effects, for reasons that are easy to understand. If we devote our lives to the welfare of others, we immediately are in harmony with virtually everyone around us. They are looking after their own welfare and we suddenly appear as an unknown friend, in Śāntideva's words. I look down right now on the town of Lone Pine in the valley below, population two thousand. They may not know it, but they have a friend. To the extent that I develop this cherishing of others, I become an unknown friend for two thousand people down there, for the animals living round about, for all sentient beings. My actions harmonize with the reality that I exist in fundamental interdependence with the rest of life.

Our lives up to this point may well have been dominated by self-centeredness, pursuing our own good to the detriment of others around us. The same attitude may well have dominated our previous lives. Our present state is the fruit of the years we have lived in this lifetime as well as the end product of countless past lives; lifetimes that encompass a bounty of self-centeredness. If we are not particularly satisfied with how we are doing right now, we may hold self-centeredness responsible. There are, however, beings who have taken a different course, bodhisattvas and Buddhas who from lifetime to lifetime have cherished others above themselves. As Śāntideva says in a wonderfully potent verse:

> What need is there to elaborate?
> Fools apply themselves to their own welfare,

While sages act for the welfare of others.
Just look at the difference between them.[2]

We work so hard at our own well-being, striving to the point of exhaustion. The Tibetan Buddhist teachers under whom I studied have frequently commented that if we gave nearly as much intelligent effort to authentic spiritual practice as we give to simply making a living, we probably would be highly advanced bodhisattvas by now, if not Buddhas.

We have allowed self-centeredness to exhaust us in the past, and in return have received very little good and a lot of anxiety. Anxiety is built into self-centeredness by necessity. As soon as we fix on *my* possessions, *my* this, *my* that, we must then be on guard to protect our turf against all other sentient beings, many of whom are also dominated by self-centeredness. Insofar as self-centeredness decreases, the anxiety and suffering will inevitably ease off.

Sechibuwa elaborates on this, and to a large extent we can confirm his findings experientially for ourselves. All mental distortions, he says—attachment, arrogance, hostility, resentment, jealousy—come from the root of self-grasping, and self-centeredness lies at the very core of this reification of our own existence. He makes the analogy that being subject to this self-centeredness is like wandering naked with a bundle of thorns on our backs. No matter where we go, no matter what we do, it gives us suffering. Whether we engage in spiritual practice or mundane activities, it is always there.

Sechibuwa advises us even to address our own self-centeredness in the following way: "Self-centeredness, I have identified you at last! You have dominated my life in the past, pretending to be my friend. You claimed to be my ally and promised me all good things, but in fact you worked to my detriment. Now that I see you I will not rest until you are completely vanquished, because you have tricked me, nestling in my mind as if to help me, while in fact you were a traitor. You

---

[2]*Bodhisattvacaryāvatāra*, VIII, 130. Here, the term *sages* specifically refers to Buddhas.

promised me happiness, but you gave me grief and anxiety and suffering, and I have had enough."

Keep in mind that we are not speaking to ourselves. Self-centeredness is not the self but rather an obscuration, or affliction, of the mind. Look for it not only in the quiet of meditation but in daily life. Remember that this comes under the topic of transforming unfavorable circumstances into the path. Use the occasions in life that cause you unhappiness to identify self-centeredness. When misfortune arises, unhappiness occurs as a response. See if you can note the role of self-centeredness in the episode and see how self-centeredness is in fact the source of the suffering. In the absence of self-centeredness an external stimulus can put a dent in your car, it can give you illness or physical pain, but it cannot give you grief or anxiety.

Sechibuwa makes another very important point. All of the Buddha's teachings, he says, and all the thousands of volumes of Indian and Tibetan commentaries are designed for one purpose only: attenuating and dispelling mental afflictions. However these afflictions are categorized, they all boil down to self-centeredness. All of Buddhadharma is about vanquishing these maladies of the mind because they lie at the root of all suffering. The Buddhas have only one task and one motivation—to lead each of us from suffering.

If we take this seriously and even consider the possibility of loosening the bonds of self-centeredness, of looking outward and offering our lives to the world, it is frightening. And this fear expresses itself so articulately in the very terms of self-centeredness, "What will become of me?" No less than climbing a high mountain or exploring uncharted regions of the ocean, setting out on this great venture takes courage and faith. But we need not go head over heels. Faith is not a drastic thing; we can take it gradually. We can put one toe in first and begin to identify for ourselves the effects of self-centeredness.

It is worth investigating for ourselves how self-centeredness has brought us harm under the guise of protecting us. We can infer that it has similarly brought us harm in the preceding lifetime and the one before that. Now expand the mind to life before life before life, each one spanning various experiences, a certain sense of personal identity, a certain way of dying. In each lifetime we have had aspirations, yearning for happiness and striving to achieve it. But as long as we fail to recognize the true enemy, then our aspirations for well-being are severely hampered. We come to this present life as the culmination of everything we have lived for in all of our lives up to this point. Unless we employ skillful means as a remedy for self-centeredness, it will keep on perpetuating itself throughout the rest of this lifetime, through the coming *bardo*, or intermediate period, into the next lifetime, and so on without end.

Self-centeredness does not vanish by itself. We will continue to suffer because of the mental distortions and unwholesome behavior that it spawns. It is not difficult to understand how self-centeredness harms us. And yet, if we look around us, we can ask in the quiet of our mind, how many people out there—let alone other kinds of sentient beings—have really recognized the extent to which self-centeredness and its resulting distortions bring them harm, discontent, anxiety, grief, and pain? How many, on the contrary, base their lives firmly upon the priority of self-centeredness and identify with attachment, confusion, and hostility, as if this were the only natural and proper way to live? Very few people have even a glimmering of the profound disadvantages that these mental distortions hold for us.

Encountering a teaching such as this may be the first opportunity in all of our lifetimes to really tackle this problem. Not that Tibetan Buddhism has a monopoly here, but the fact remains that this text offers an exceptionally clear elucidation of the nature of self-centeredness and the manner in which it harms us. Not only does it identify this, which is a major step in itself, but it then offers us means to counteract this deep-rooted malady.

As we begin to make an effort, we may quickly become discouraged and feel that it is not really possible to counteract self-centeredness. We may wilt at the thought, ''My neural circuits are so conditioned to self-centeredness that I just cannot escape the pattern.'' It feels like self-centeredness has us well in its clutches and is firmly in control. After all, it has had a very long time to embed itself in our psyches. The results will be gradual as we counteract the conditioning of our mental, verbal, and physical behavior. At the same time, the results of skillful efforts are manifest, and we can experience them right in this lifetime.

If we take this seriously as a profoundly meaningful way to vanquish self-centeredness in our lives and to cultivate a loving concern for others, it becomes a central feature in our aspirations and our value system. It continues throughout this lifetime as an orientation, even if, at the end of this life, we still have a considerable amount of self-centeredness left. Nevertheless, a current is established that in all likelihood will continue building momentum. In the next lifetime it will be easier insofar as we have made effective efforts in this lifetime. How many lifetimes it takes depends upon the skill, the intelligence, and continuity of practice. If we dabble at it casually and intermittently, it will obviously take longer. But it is also possible to overcome self-centeredness in this very lifetime and become a bodhisattva.

Blame everything on one thing. Gradually or swiftly, it is an effective means to counteract self-centeredness and end this source of misery, strife, and anxiety. Until we do, there is no question that it will continue endlessly.

Meditate on great kindness toward everyone.

Sechibuwa's notes bring this next verse right into the most difficult area of the practice. He encourages us to cultivate a sense of loving kindness and compassion towards those who bring us harm.

To do so, we must stand back from the situation. Resentment and ill-will can be generated by a single incident or by a long sequence of events. Recognize that in the broad view this hostile relationship is something quite temporary and depends on changing causal circumstances. Obviously, at some point this person was not our enemy. We might even have been friends. Who can say how a relationship may change, even within this lifetime? A simple unkind remark, a discourtesy, an act of thoughtlessness can so easily trigger resentment, and yet a single act of kindness can just as easily spark a friendship. The person we now regard as an enemy may turn around and do us some service or simply be friendly. We may even find that we have built a whole scenario in our minds and that this person does not really dislike us at all.

Sechibuwa puts this in a larger perspective, recognizing that this person also exists as a continuum and has experienced previous lives. Having come in contact in this lifetime, there is an extremely high probability, if not certainty, that we have been in a relationship before. If we did know each other in the preceding life, there is no guarantee that our relationship then was one of animosity rather than kindness. This person might have been a mother or a father to us. Recognizing the mutability of relationships, we can infer that, whatever harm this person has done to us in this lifetime, in past lifetimes he or she has on many more occasions protected us from harm and brought us happiness. As true as this has been in the past, it may also be true in the future. Cultivate loving kindness in this way.

These practices are accessible only if we have confidence in the continuity of consciousness from one lifetime to another and in the karma that relates these lifetimes meaningfully. But if we do have this confidence, it is important to use it to transform our lives and our attitudes. Here is a way to derive some real benefit from belief in facets of reality which for the time being are closed to direct experience. Likewise, we can recognize that the suffering this enemy has brought us can only have resulted from our own unwholesome actions in the past. We cannot experience suffering unless we have planted its seeds. Like ourselves, this person has mental distortions. The force of our karma has prodded this persons' mental distortions, compelling him to engage in hostile speech or action. Granted, if he had no mental distortions, we could not possibly prod him into unwholesome actions. But assuming he does, our own karma lies at the root of his hostility.

Again and again, think of mental distortions as afflictions, contrary to nature. When someone is hot-tempered, narrow-minded, bigoted, selfish, or thoughtless, we think, "What a disgusting person!" But all these qualities are afflictions, and that person is the first to bear the initial brunt of suffering from them. The more repugnant a person is, the more likely that person is to be suffering from the mental distortions that render him or her repugnant to us.

In these ways we seek to cultivate loving kindness and compassion for people who, as a result of mental afflictions, have brought us harm and whom we therefore identify as our enemies. The next step of the meditation is to practice the taking and sending in this context. We begin by taking from our enemy those unwholesome and distorted qualities that we find repugnant. We take them into our heart in the form of black smoke, and then imagine offering ourselves completely to this person: our body, our possessions, and our merits.

Sechibuwa expands on this: cultivate the sense of having offered your body as a servant, not only to your enemy but to all sentient beings in general. Śāntideva also makes this point strongly in the eighth chapter of the *Guide to the Bodhisattva's Way of Life.* Once it is offered, he says, this body can no longer be mine, obtaining things for me and manipulating other people to my benefit. In your mind's eye, call all sentient beings together, with the people who have harmed you in the forefront, and say, "I offer my body to you to do with as you please." From this point on it belongs to them, and how they use it—or even misuse it—is up to them. Granted that this is a potentially dangerous practice, it is our responsibility and our challenge to figure out how to use it intelligently. The point lies in seeing ourselves as an instrument for the service of others.

Having engaged in this Mind Training, we can recognize that a person who has harmed us thereby kicks us out of our complacency and pushes us into practice. If we are surrounded by friends, our mental distortions may rarely be triggered and we can easily exaggerate our sense of the progress we have made in our practice. But when hostility triggers animosity, it is like a bucket full of cold water in the face, making it very clear that we have something here to work on.

When someone harms us or otherwise repels us, we can simply say, "This will pass," and distract ourselves with happier thoughts, turning our minds away. But this leaves us no less vulnerable the next time around. Suppose, for example, that Joe is a particularly arrogant person who rubs us the wrong way. We avoid having anything to do with him. After a while he changes jobs, or moves away, and we have no more contact with him. Joe gradually fades from our mind and no longer triggers our hostility. Now Jack appears and he is just as arrogant. Exactly the same thing happens, because nothing has been learned.

What Joe and Jack are doing is offering us an opportunity for self-knowledge, and at the same time providing an impetus for putting this training into practice. We can meditate authentically on the kindness of the very person who harms us and cultivate our awareness of this.

The kindness of a service rendered, or a gift, large or small, is a limited kindness. It may ease our suffering temporarily, but it does not render our minds less vulnerable to suffering. The greatest kindness another person can show us is to help transform our minds so that contentment arises more readily from the nature of the mind itself, without pleasant stimuli. A Dharma teacher or a spiritual friend can do that. Our enemies can as well. They show us the truest, innermost kindness, and without them the teachings of books and spiritual friends are insufficient for our spiritual growth. We need these people. They serve an indispensable role in our lives. And what do they get out of it? Nothing, at best. They receive no benefit from the act of giving us harm, and if they are doing something really unwholesome, they get nothing but misfortune. There is ground here for both gratitude and compassion.

Sechibuwa then makes an even more emphatic statement. Inasmuch as the inflictors of harm are truly aiding our practice, they are great friends and helpers in our spiritual growth, and in this sense, we can regard them gladly and from our hearts as emanations of our spiritual mentor or of the Buddha.

Sechibuwa goes on to speak of harms, such as illness, that have no particular inflictor. Poor health certainly fades some of our enchantment with the pleasures of mundane life. It sobers us up and may encourage us to face some of the deeper issues of our existence. In the proper context, illness may indeed encourage us to cultivate renunciation, recognizing that the pleasures we experience result from external stimuli and are fundamentally unsatisfactory. A life that is focused on the acquisition of such pleasant stimuli is continually vulnerable to suffering. If we have sufficient understanding, illness can deepen our incentive to transform our minds and hearts in ways that are deeply manifest.

If there is no suffering, then there is no renunciation, no aspiration to emerge from mental distortions and a way of life pervaded by dissatisfaction. I do not believe that suffering matures us by itself. My knowledge of history and my own experience persuade me that it is patently untrue that a person who suffers a lot automatically becomes a better person. Suffering alone is not sufficient: an intelligent, insightful response to the suffering is needed. With these two together, Dharma *and* suffering, we can definitely grow through a wholesome transformation.

Sechibuwa mentions another potential advantage of suffering. It can attenuate conceit and arrogance. It is hard to be arrogant if we are suffering a lot. Moreover, at the very root of the bodhisattva practice lies compassion. Where we ourselves have suffered, whether in personal relationships or in solitude, in physical pain, depression, anxiety, or grief, we have a ground for sympathizing with others in similar situations. We can extrapolate, recognizing in others our own yearning to be free of suffering. Without this it may be very difficult to feel empathy, looking down on others as if observing a different species, scratching one's head and wondering what they are so upset about.

As we learn to respond to suffering in these ways, then the very experience of suffering, in the light of this Dharma practice, is a means for overcoming suffering. Once we are able to do this, says Sechibuwa, all our activities of body, speech, and mind are transformed into wholesome actions. In descriptions of the bodhisattva path (without considering tantra), it is from this point that a bodhisattva's career begins its three countless eons culminating in full enlightenment.

Meditation on the deceptive appearances of the Four Bodies is unsurpassed in guarding emptiness.

Up to this point, the discussion of transforming unfavorable circumstances into the path has focused on relative bodhicitta. Now the author moves on to consider this transformation in the context of training in ultimate bodhicitta. This verse, which appears in Chekawa's root text but not in later versions, obviously needs explanation. Sechibuwa begins by focusing on the idea that the entire cycle of existence, all causes and effects, every being who is harmed and each one that inflicts harm, all phenomena both inner and environmental, are nothing more than appearances of our own mind.

Such a mind-boggling statement ought not to be swallowed without chewing. Sechibuwa assumes that we already have some background in the teachings on emptiness and understand what is meant, and also what is not meant, by "deceptive appearances." Without this context, the literal statement could easily be seen as an expression of solipsism. But in fact, this view that emptiness and phenomena exist together as dependently related events takes a "middle way" between the extremes of solipsism and nihilism on the one hand and realism on the other.

The point is that these phenomena are merely appearances, but have no ultimate existence whatsoever. In this sense they are like pure, unblemished space. We ourselves, as well as the inflictor of harm and the person who is harmed, are all empty of intrinsic existence.

Sechibuwa's explanation of the "Four Bodies" presents an unusual interpretation of these terms. The first, *dharmakāya*, is sometimes translated as the Truth Body. In this particular context, *dharmakāya* is understood as the absence of intrinsic birth and existence of all phenomena: that phenomena neither arise nor exist autonomously of their own accord. Whatever has no intrinsic birth or existence can have no intrinsic cessation. This lack of intrinsic cessation is called *sambhoga-kāya*, roughly translated as the Enjoyment Body of the Buddha. If phenomena are empty of intrinsic arising and intrinsic cessation, there can be no intermediate period of abiding in existence, and that very lack of abiding or dwelling, is called here *nirmānakāya*, or the Emanation Body. Such phenomena then are not real: not intrinsically existent in the past, present, or future. This lack of inherent reality is called *svabhā-vakāya*, or the Nature Body.

Thus, nothing has any existence apart from the Four Bodies: neither illness, nor one's own mind, nor any inflictor of harm, nor any cause, nor any effect. In this way we can regard all phenomena, including every thought that arises, as the Four Bodies. Granted, it takes considerable background to practice this with understanding rather than simply as if following a formula.

The supreme method entails four practices.

In the next verse, Sechibuwa moves from the training of thoughts in transforming unfavorable circumstances to another approach: training in terms of action.

1.Accumulating the collections. There are two types of collections: the collection of merit and the collection of wisdom. The collection of merit culminates in the attainment of the body of a Buddha; the collection of wisdom in the attainment of a Buddha's mind.

We can collect merit by cultivating faith in, and make offerings to, the Buddha, Dharma, and Saṃgha and to our spiritual mentor. Taking refuge, developing bodhicitta, donating to the poor—all of these are ways to accumulate the spiritual power that is needed for growth, both in terms of compassion and wisdom. We accumulate the "collection of wisdom" by cultivating understanding and insight by means of study, reflection, and meditation.

If we skip this first aspect of spiritual practice—of faith, service, and devotion—with the intention of becoming enlightened through insight alone, we don't stand a chance. Merit is the juice that enables the meditation to effectively transform the heart and mind. Some people meditate for short periods of time and have great realizations; others meditate for a long time and have only problems. It is the accumulated spiritual momentum of merit that makes the difference, not how determined we are, or how austere, how many hours we meditate, or how much pain we tolerate.

People bemoan the fact that their lives are too busy to practice; obligations leave little time for meditation, retreats, and study. If we truly wish to practice, and at the same time have obligations we cannot responsibly relinquish, what can we do?

First, it is important to realize that these obligations are not permanent, but another phase of practice. Later, changing circumstances will allow us to change the nature of our spiritual practice. But another very important opportunity is frequently overlooked in the West, largely because the whole notion of contemplative practice within a mystical tradition is alien to our culture. Those who are not able to meditate intensively can help those who are. Offering service in this way enhances our own practice, gradually building up the spiritual power that will enable us to succeed when the time comes to meditate seriously. If we are fortunate enough to have a spiritual mentor, it is appropriate to offer service. It could be something as simple as vacuuming the floor. If we have Dharma friends, or know of a monk or a nun, or some Tibetans in India whom we believe to be practicing earnestly at a depth inaccessible to us under the present circumstances, it is ap-

propriate to support them with money and with service. Many
people who work full time have surplus funds, and this is a
meaningful way to spend them.

Although this is a valid practice in itself, it is no substitute
for more active practice. The Mind Training is in many respects
ideal for busy people, because it can be implemented again
and again in daily life. This is an ideal way to accumulate the
proper internal circumstances that will enable us to succeed
when our external circumstances are finally conducive to serious meditation.

Sechibuwa then directs us to a series of familiar but very
potent statements with which we can genuinely offer up our
lives. In illness, for example, the prayer takes the shape: "If
it benefits others that I am ill, may I be ill. If it benefits others
that I recover, may I recover. If it benefits others that I now
perish, may I perish. If it benefits others that I live long, may
I have a long life. Whatever happens, if it benefits others, may
it be."

He is not prescribing apathy. On the contrary, this takes great
courage and, at the same time, humility. We don't know what
the future holds, long term or short, but we can simply offer
our life on principle: "Whatever is of greatest benefit to others,
may this be." Imagine having had a chronic ailment for years
and years. It is natural to get very impatient to be free of it.
But it is useful to ask, "What are the potential benefits of this
illness?" We don't know what lessons have yet to be learned
from the experience of this chronic ailment. So with whatever courage we can muster, we can cultivate the aspiration
that whatever is of greatest benefit to others, may it be. Such
a prayer or aspiration is an extremely effective means for cutting off hope and anxiety.

2.Purifying the unwholesome. In the past we have engaged
in unwholesome physical, verbal, and mental actions. All these
actions are of the past and cannot be touched; we cannot reach
back and wipe them away. They have left detrimental imprints
on our mind-stream that obstruct our spiritual practice and
manifest as suffering when they come to full maturation, giv-

ing rise to misfortune and grief. However, these imprints can be affected, and even purified, by our present behavior. They are like seeds carried along in the current of our mind-stream. We cannot annihilate them without a trace, but we can burn them so that they have little or no potency to cause damaging results.

For this purpose we need the four remedial powers. The first of these powers is oriented to the past. With a sense of regret, recognize the deed as unwholesome and unfortunate. Acknowledge that it would have been better not to bring suffering to ourselves and others in this way. The second power is oriented to the present and future. Resolve to avoid the deed totally in the future, or if the pattern is deeply ingrained and will engage us again in spite of our best efforts, then resolve to avoid it as much as possible until it is gradually and completely dispelled from our behavior. The third of the four powers is the power of reliance. An unwholesome action directed to our spiritual mentor, or to the Buddha, Dharma, or Saṃgha, can be purified by taking refuge and committing ourselves once again to the enlightened beings. If we have acted in an unwholesome way towards other sentient beings, the power of reliance means cultivating bodhicitta more fully. The last of the four powers consists of purificatory activities. For example, we can begin to purify imprints from the act of killing by going out of our way to save lives. If in our youth we killed when fishing, we might go to a restaurant where fish are kept in a tank to be killed for food. Buying the fish and releasing them in water where they could survive would be a purificatory activity. There are also many meditations specifically designed to purify the mind from unwholesome imprints, such as the Vajrasattva purificatory meditation with the hundred-syllable *mantra*.

There is no evil so great that its imprints cannot be purified. However, as long as they are not purified through these remedial powers they invariably create problems for our spiritual practice, especially in deeper meditation. And they yield full suffering when they come to maturation.

3. Making offering to spirits. Almost all contemplative traditions hold the firm conviction that animals and human beings share this world with a variety of spirits. Some of these non-human entities are malevolent and can inflict harm upon us, so traditional Buddhists practice making offerings to them. Sechibuwa instructs us to imagine these inflictors of harm before us in the form of *devas*, or gods. He then describes a practice that is suitable only for those who are well advanced along the path. Imagine these malevolent spirits as wonderful beings of celestial light, and address them in this way: "You have encouraged me to practice the two types of bodhicitta, and because of this you have helped me in finding happiness and dispelling suffering. I request you, who are so kind, please do not cure my illnesses, but let them last for a long time."

In this way we cut out all hope and fear, all anxiety over misfortune. It takes a very strong practitioner of Mind Training to transform these calamities into the path. For those of us who are not quite up to this, Sechibuwa suggests we also make offerings to these malevolent entities but focus instead on cultivating loving kindness and compassion towards them. Address them, saying, "You have created obstacles for my practice, which is dedicated to all sentient beings. This will bring you disadvantages and you will be reborn in the hell realm as a result. I wish to help you, I make offerings to you, and I think of you with benevolence. So please do not harm me."

4. Making offerings to the dharmapālas. These are non-human entities who, far from being malevolent, protect the Dharma and support spiritual practitioners. Make offerings to them and ask them to protect us from obstacles in our practice. Address them, saying, "You, who have committed yourselves in the presence of the Buddhas to support the Dharma, please help as you have promised."

Whatever you encounter, immediately apply it to meditation.

Sechibuwa comments that the preceding verses are the actual teachings of the third point on transforming unfavorable circumstances into the path. This final verse of the third point is a contemplative practice to be implemented between formal sessions, as we are out and about in daily life.

Whatever misfortune, calamity, or suffering arises, whether you are mugged or robbed or thrown in jail, immediately apply it to the Mind Training. Recall that there are countless sentient beings who are experiencing similar misfortune, and practice taking the misfortune of others upon yourself and into your own self-centeredness. Likewise, when you see others in misfortune, imagine in your mind's eye taking this upon yourself. Whenever a strong mental affliction such as attachment or anger arises, practice in the same way: think of the innumerable sentient beings who are subject to the same affliction and take it upon yourself.

We can see that the transformation of unfavorable circumstances is intimately tied to attenuating and finally ending these mental afflictions. Until we stop these perpetual hopes and anxieties over momentary shifts in fortune, we cannot possibly transform unfavorable circumstances into the path. On the other hand, once we really do transcend these temporal polarities of fear and hope, we will have made a crooked stick into a straight one.

The Fourth Point
A Synthesis of Practice for One Life

As is frequently found in Buddhism, this fourth point synthesizes a wide variety of practices into a few principles. By first familiarizing ourselves with the individual practices, and then drawing back into the synthesis, it becomes practical to implement these teachings in the course of daily life.

To synthesize the essence of this practical guidance, apply yourself to the five powers.

1. The power of resolution. Looking forward with determination, we resolve not to be parted from the cultivation of the two bodhicittas, relative and ultimate, until our full awakening. We resolve not to abandon this practice for as long as we live; not for this entire day, not for this entire month, not for this entire year. We can establish this continuity of mind most earnestly when we appreciate the depth and magnificence of these two qualities of mind: ultimate bodhicitta that probes into the nature of reality with such depth, and relative bodhicitta, born of loving kindness and compassion, that aspires to full awakening for the benefit of all creatures. Until these two are brought to culmination, we resolve never to be parted from the practice of cultivating them.

2. *The power of familiarization.* Looking to the present rather than the future, the author encourages us never to be distracted from the cultivation of ultimate and relative bodhicitta. Profound spiritual transformation occurs only with persistent practice, for it is through familiarizing ourselves with fresh ways of viewing reality and fresh ways of responding to situations that old, harmful patterns are broken up. Sudden breakthroughs, such as a vivid insight, are certainly meaningful experiences on the spiritual path, but unless they are sustained through the power of familiarization, their long-term influence on our lives is bound to be quite limited.

3. *The power of the white seed.* Imagine our present practice as a seed for spiritual growth, white in its virtue and wholesomeness, which when mature will transform into the tree of awakening. Cultivate this seed by welcoming any opportunity to transform unfavorable circumstances into spiritual growth. We can cultivate it by engaging in wholesome actions and accumulating merit, and especially by using our body and possessions to do whatever brings the greatest blessing. With so many options presented, we need to seek out what is most meaningful for the cultivation of these bodhicittas and then strive in that.

4. *The power of abandonment.* In this practice what is being abandoned is self-grasping. We are reminded again that since beginningless time beyond all imagination, self-grasping has lain at the very core of all mental distortions and afflictions. It has brought us to unfavorable rebirths and is responsible for all the undesirable circumstances that we encounter. It is self-centeredness that obstructs realization and prevents us from deriving the full benefit from our spiritual practice. Recognize when self-grasping manifests in daily life. It is important to notice it especially at times of passion, when we are aroused or irritated, and try not to succumb to it for even a moment.

I mentioned before that self-centeredness can be overcome only gradually because it is so deeply ingrained in our minds and behavior. But it is also true that if we focus right in the moment and recognize self-centeredness, it is often not so difficult to reject. To be free of self-centeredness continuously for a whole year may be difficult, but a moment is easy. Not only in negative terms but positively, we can be sensitive right in the present to the needs of others, sensitive to things that make others happy, be it a small gift, an act of service, or simply a friendly gaze. For a moment we can become a very brief but good facsimile of a bodhisattva. And the more of these moments we can saturate with the cherishing of others, the more we are molding ourselves into the bodhisattvas that we will become.

5. *The power of prayer.* Like the dedication of merit, this is a directing of the spiritual momentum of merit that we have accumulated by engaging in wholesome behavior. One prayer that is strongly encouraged here is to dedicate the fruits of our practice for all future lives, so that ultimate and relative bodhicitta may continually increase. For all our lifetimes until our full awakening, pray that we may never be separated from these two bodhicittas.

In essence, the prayer is that we will be intelligent and skillful enough to bring any unfavorable circumstance into our spiritual practice. It is easy to pray that we avoid misfortune, grief, or calamity, but to pray for the skill and fortitude to bring these circumstances onto the path is very courageous. This and future lifetimes are not likely to be completely free of calamity, nor would this be optimal for our spiritual growth. So we can pray, "May I have the wisdom to recognize the situation and, be it ever so unfortunate or miserable, apply to it my wisdom and my enthusiasm for Dharma, for my own welfare and for others."

Along with this prayer, we are encouraged to make offerings to our spiritual mentor, to the Buddha, Dharma, and Samgha, to our meditation deities, and to the *dharmapālas*, or Dharma protectors. And we can pray to these beings also, "May I never be separated from the two bodhicittas."

The next prayer that Sechibuwa mentions is especially poignant: "May I always encounter holy spiritual mentors who teach this Dharma." I am moved when I look at the lives of people who have no apparent spiritual orientation or practice, but are simply focused on just getting by, taking vacations, making money or a reputation. I am also saddened to meet people who have recognized their spiritual need but have not found an authentic guide. They may follow a guru who has little to offer, or pick up books indiscriminately, without distinguishing between the mediocre and a text that represents years of experience by a highly realized being. But any teacher or teaching that can authentically show the means of cultivating ultimate and relative bodhicitta represents the essence of the Buddhadharma. If the teaching emphasizes refining the mind so that it is capable of realizing ultimate truth and cherishing others with loving kindness and compassion, we are on the right track.

The Mahāyāna teaching on transferring consciousness is just these precious five powers.

At the end of a life devoted to Dharma, there comes a time for rounding off the practice. When we recognize that illness or simply old age has brought us very close to death, we can implement specific practices to influence the transfer of consciousness from this life to the next. The Tibetans have preserved a number of such practices, called *phowa*, working with energies associated with the transfer of consciousness. These practices are taught in the context of Buddhist tantra, and they are often explained in relation to the *bardo* (the period following death and before the next life), as set forth, for instance, in the *Tibetan Book of the Dead*. But not many people are fully qualified to practice tantra. Many of these practices require a high degree of spiritual maturity; before we can authentically engage in tantric practices such as phowa, we should already have made considerable progress in developing mental and emotional stability, and ultimate and relative bodhicitta.

The whole issue of death and dying, both for ourselves and for loved ones, is a popular topic now, addressed by secular and religious teachers from various traditions. The phowa practice based on the five powers presented here in the Mahāyāna context of the Mind Training is a non-tantric bodhisattva practice, which is more accessible for most people. We can keep this very practical and precious teaching in mind not only for ourselves, but also for loved ones who are not Buddhists, let alone advanced tantric practitioners. Reading the *Tibetan Book of the Dead* to a dying friend who is not interested in Buddhism will not likely be very helpful; sharing this practice may well be useful.

The state of mind just prior to death is most influential for determining the very next lifetime. Bringing our mind into a very wholesome state at this crucial time does not wipe out all the unwholesome actions that have gone before, but it does provide the most direct impetus for the rebirth immediately following. Conversely, if one should be so unfortunate as to die with an unwholesome mind, such as rage, this may well lead to an unfortunate existence in the next life. Once again, this does not mean that all the merit and favorable imprints accumulated through life are wasted, but they may be postponed for a lifetime or longer.

This method of transferring consciousness into favorable circumstances in the very next life entails five powers that go by the same names as the five powers mentioned in the preceding verse, but here they have different meanings.

1. The power of the white seed. Once again, we are cultivating a white seed of virtue, which is interpreted here as release from attachment to our body and possessions. The Tibetan contemplative Gen Lamrimpa was once teaching this and chuckling as he spoke of how people acquire things, use them for a short time, then die and are reborn completely naked; then spend another life acquiring possessions only to die again, dead broke. On the threshold of death, if we are so fortunate as to anticipate its approach, it is very important to loosen our attachment to possessions: not only to give them away, but to really release them from our minds. We can give them as offerings to our spiritual mentor, to the Saṃgha, to our fellow Dharma practitioners, or to the poor. It hardly needs to be said that we should not leave the dregs of our belongings to those who have been kind to us. For our own welfare, we should release these attachments as we face death, and be free of them. They are no longer ours to use.

When death comes, we have used up even our body. Śāntideva tells us to regard the body as a loan for the duration of our lives, for us to use as an instrument in the service of others. Parts deteriorate from old age, or the whole may be crushed suddenly in an accident. Either way, it is time to release it and not to cling.

We can start practicing this now. The very strong attachment that we generally have to the body is what makes us so vulnerable to its suffering. After freeing attachment, the author continues, generate the mind of fearlessness. We ourselves create much of the fear that surrounds death through our attachment to what we have to leave: our loved ones, our children, our possessions, our homeland, all the familiar things we are accustomed to. See if, during the course of life, we can enjoy these things but release the clinging to them. If we can really set aside the attachment, especially just before death, we allow ourselves the freedom to dispense with a lot of fear, and more so if our lives have been devoted to Dharma to the best of our ability. We then have very little reason to be afraid.

2. *The power of prayer.* If we regret any unwholesome actions when we are about to die, this is the time to disclose or confess them and apply the four remedial powers explained under the third point. After purifying the mind, take refuge. Recognize that there is a source on which we can rely: the Buddha, the Dharma, the Saṃgha, the spiritual mentor. We are encouraged to make offerings in our mind's eye to the Triple Gem and to the Dharma protectors, praying: "May I remember and practice the two bodhicittas in the intermediate period between death and the next rebirth. May there be continuity, that I may meet in the next life with a holy spiritual mentor

who teaches Dharma. I place my hope in you; make my way to joy a straight and clear one." Prayer is extremely important at this time, and will strongly influence the nature of one's death, the bardo, and the next life.

3. *The power of abandonment.* Recognize the self-grasping that clings to the body and to the self. Recognize that this fundamental distortion of the mind is responsible for the suffering that surrounds death, and as long as we remain subject to this self-grasping there is no true joy. Reject this clinging to the body and self for the remainder of this lifetime and in the coming bardo.

4. *The power of resolution.* This is not merely a prayer but a firm resolve to recollect the two bodhicittas during the approaching bardo: to recollect, on the one hand, the illusory nature of the experiences to come—that they are deceptive appearances of the mind and not intrinsically existent—and, on the other hand, to recollect and practice relative bodhicitta in this time. Just prior to death, bring this to mind again and again with firm resolve.

5. *The power of familiarization.* Sechibuwa points out here that the most important thing is to familiarize ourselves with the cultivation of the two bodhicittas without interruption throughout this life. Now, as this life draws to a close, he explains the most favorable posture in which to die. Lie on your right side, with your right hand under the right cheek, your little finger closing off the right nostril, and breathe through the left nostril. Because of its influence on the subtle energies coursing through the body, this is an excellent posture for engaging in the other meditations prior to death. In this posture, engage in the practice of taking and sending conjoined with the breath. Inhaling through the left nostril, draw the suffering and the sources of suffering of all sentient beings into your heart, vanquishing self-centeredness. As you exhale, send out white light of purity and loving kindness to all sentient beings and imagine it bringing them whatever they require: food, clothing, wealth, or spiritual teaching. Imagine them receiving all that they need and want.

The author also speaks of a meditation in the same posture for the cultivation of ultimate bodhicitta just before death, which he encourages us to practice alternately with the taking and sending. This is a crucial time to recognize that all of existence, be it saṃsāra or *nirvāṇa*, consists of appearances to the mind that are not intrinsically existent. Recall that your own Buddha nature is not ultimately different from the mind of the Buddha and recognize the essentially divine nature of your own mind. Allow your mind to relax in this sphere of ultimate reality and, holding this awareness right to the point of death, recognize that for this ultimate nature there is no transference of consciousness; there is no motion.

The Fifth Point
The Measure of Having Trained the Mind

The fifth point concerns how we measure our progress in the Mind Training. What are the indications that the practice is working successfully?

All Dharma is included in one purpose.

Through hearing, reflection, and meditation, we explore the issue of personal identity and, as Sechibuwa says, we find upon investigation that this "I" as an intrinsic entity, existing independently of conceptual designation, is no more real than the horns of a hare. Since beginningless time, this illusion has brought us suffering and discontent. Seeking to be free of the suffering and to find greater meaning and fulfillment in our lives, we practice Dharma. Many of us have by now encountered a wide range of practices—breath awareness, mindfulness, loving kindness, the Lam Rim practices, meditation on emptiness, meditative quiescence, and even tantric practices. All these practices, all the teachings of the Buddha, all the commentaries, serve one purpose: to subdue self-grasping.

We are now challenged to investigate for ourselves the quality of our lives, and to see how our actions of body, speech, and mind have influenced the level of our self-grasping. We may find that the practice is in fact enhancing the so-called eight mundane concerns—pleasure and pain, gain and loss, praise and blame, honor and dishonor. If our practice does not diminish self-grasping, or perhaps even enhances it, then no matter how austere and determined we are, no matter how many hours a day we devote to learning, reflection, and meditation, our spiritual practice is in vain.

A close derivative of self-grasping is the feeling of self-importance. Such arrogance or pride is a very dangerous pitfall for people practicing Dharma. Especially in Tibetan Buddhism, with its many levels of practice, the exalted aspirations of the bodhisattva path, and the mystery surrounding initiation into tantra, we may easily feel part of an elite. Moreover, the philosophy of Buddhism is so subtly refined and so penetrating that, as we gain an understanding of it, this also can give rise to intellectual pride.

But if these are the results of the practice, then something has gone awry. Recall the well-known saying among Tibetan Buddhists that a pot with a little water in it makes a loud noise when shaken, but a pot full of water makes no noise at all. People with very little realization often want to tell everyone about the insights they have experienced, the bliss and subtleties of their meditation, and how it has radically transformed their life. But those who are truly steeped in realization do not feel compelled to advertise it, and instead simply dwell in that realization. They are concerned not to describe their own progress, but to direct the awareness of others to ways in which their own hearts and minds can be awakened.

As Tibetan wisdom points out, vegetation does not grow on top of a high mountain, but grows luxuriously in the valleys; and, similarly, a person who feels superior to others learns very little from them and assumes they have nothing to offer someone so far above them. But a person who looks up to others, not just intellectually but from the heart, is ready to listen to their wisdom. And just as the valley accumulates the good top soil from above, so likewise this person is receptive to wisdom, again and again.

Although we all try to engage in spiritual practice according to our own abilities, it is very helpful to have some criterion by which we can estimate our progress. Here is the crucial test: how has our sense of personal identity been influenced? The stronger our self-grasping, the more easily it gives rise to irritation, anger, and resentment. It gives rise also to attachment, and actually forms the basis of self-centeredness. We can check the level of our own self-grasping by checking on the derivative mental distortions and obscurations that arise from its root.

On a more optimistic note, if we find that our practice results in decreased self-grasping, we can recognize its authenticity. This too distinguishes a true Dharma practitioner from one who is merely practicing a facsimile. Keep in mind that one can be a great scholar and articulate speaker, or spend many hours in meditation, without being an authentic Dharma practitioner at all.

Maintain the chief of the two witnesses.

The two witnesses are others and oneself, and both have some value. It is worthwhile to heed other people's estimation of us, but, as Sechibuwa swiftly points out, it is not the chief of the two witnesses. We can pull the wool over other people's eyes, either intentionally or unintentionally by showing our best side regardless of what is going on inside. Others are to be taken into account, but the chief witness is our own internal awareness. With careful, honest introspection we can judge the quality not only of our physical and verbal behavior, but also of our own private mental activity. We ourselves are the principal witness of whether our Mind Training is authentic and working properly.

Rely continually on mental happiness alone.

We can judge whether our practice is fruitful and the Mind Training is succeeding if, regardless of whatever unfavorable circumstances occur, we respond with the antidote of cultivating the two bodhicittas, and satisfied with that, we do not become discouraged or depressed, nor respond with unwholesome action. In other words, we are encouraged to measure how constantly we reside in a state of cheerful equanimity.

As we become accustomed to the practice of taking and sending, when suffering comes to us we can see this also as evidence of the practice succeeding and be satisfied that we are taking the mental or physical suffering of others upon ourselves. After a while, the practice of transforming unfavorable circumstances into the path becomes spontaneous. We find ourselves knowing naturally how to apply each circumstance to the path, and this provides an ongoing state of contentment that is not contingent upon pleasant external stimuli. A skilled horseman does not fall off his horse even when his mind wanders or he drowses. Likewise, when we are very familiar with the Mind Training, we do not fall into a depression or unwholesome responses as soon as we meet with abuse or contempt. Instead, the mind rises spontaneously to the occasion and uses the opportunity to cultivate bodhicitta.

As we examine our practice by these measures, if we find that they do describe our present state, this does not mean that the work is finished. It simply means that we have learned how to do the practice; the task is then to become more skillful and continue to refine the mind. The Seven-Point Mind Training really synthesizes the core of the Mahāyāna Buddhist teachings of the bodhisattva path. Some of the practices are very difficult, others are more readily accessible. But it is important to estimate how we are doing, and on this path it is possible.

Other paths that are aimed at "sudden awakening" lead one on an unmapped journey that may offer no clear indications of progress. In contrast, in this practice we have definite signposts along the way. Look at your mental distortions and see how they are doing. After practicing for a month, a year, six years, are the mental distortions somewhat diminished? Do wholesome qualities arise more readily, more frequently, more deeply? At the very root of the mental distortions, is the self-grasping attenuated? Is there less self-centeredness and greater humility? Is there more loving concern for the welfare of others? All of these are causes that lead either to well-being or to misery.

Another sure sign comes from ourselves, our chief witness. How do we feel? Are we more contented people now than before we began the practice? This is especially useful if we can look back over a couple of years or so. Is our mind more cheerful, more serene? If we can answer yes, then the practice is working. Its purpose is to give us greater happiness and to lead us to awakening so that we can be of greater service to others. Indeed, the fruit of the practice is happiness and good cheer, not in some longed-for day in the future, but right during the practice itself. Although at times it is difficult, because the circumstances are difficult, the practice itself should not generally be arduous. The sign of a fruitful spiritual practice is the attenuation of mental distress.

The Sixth Point
The Pledges of Mind Training

The sixth point of the Seven-Point Mind Training concerns specific pledges. How we regard these suggested resolutions determines to a large extent how effective they are in bringing about a wholesome transformation in our life.

Think of these pledges as prescriptions that a skilled and compassionate doctor might set forth for a patient with a physical illness. In addition to medication, the doctor makes suggestions for diet and behavior, amounting perhaps to a fairly long list: avoid coffee and fat for the next two months, eat more fruit and green vegetables, exercise regularly, and so forth. The doctor's counsel comes not in the form of commandments, but helpful suggestions. The patient who ignores the list will not be punished, but simply does not benefit as the doctor intended, and the suffering of the illness continues.

This is generally the tone, in the teachings of the Buddha, for the injunctions for behavior known as *samaya*. Insofar as we abide by them, they will be to our benefit; contravening them will do us harm. They are commitments that have been found helpful, and we take them upon ourselves to enhance our own well-being. Not one of the pledges of the Seven-Point

Mind Training is confined to a specific culture or society. They are as relevant for Americans living in the twentieth century as for Tibetans living in the twelfth century.

Always practice the three principles.

1. Not to contravene any commitments we have already made in our spiritual practice: If we are following the Buddhist path for spiritual growth, we make commitments as a consequence of taking refuge in the Buddha, the Dharma, and the Saṃgha. Many of us have taken the five lay precepts, and possibly bodhisattva and tantric precepts as well, if we have received tantric initiation. There are also the ten wholesome actions to be followed and ten unwholesome actions to be avoided. The author here emphasizes that, even if the Mind Training becomes the central core of our practice, it does not substitute for other commitments that we have taken upon ourselves, or allow us to ignore them.

Essentially this concerns ethics and morality, which are said to be the basis on which all spiritual practice is founded. Without a morally wholesome way of life, nothing we do can lead to awakening—not *yoga*, or *prānāyāma*, or *samādhi*, or high tantric practice. Let's not try to build a house on sand. Whatever commitments we make, let us keep them for our own sake and for that of others.

2. Not to allow our Mind Training to become ostentatious: As we develop greater courage in this practice and become skilled at transforming unfavorable circumstances, we may as a result become overconfident, ostentatiously seeking out dangerous situations. Is it the power of our compassion that leads us to risk contagious disease in order to be of service, for example, or is it the desire to show off the superiority of our attainment? Avoid this false sense of invulnerability.

3. Not to let the Mind Training become lopsided: Imagine a very strong Dharma practitioner who, when strangers insult her, cheat her, or harm her in any way, practices the essence of the Mind Training very well. She easily transforms these unfavorable circumstances by cultivating patience, loving kindness, and compassion. On the other hand, she has less inclination to practice Dharma with those with whom she comes into frequent contact. For her husband, children, and immediate relatives, she has less tolerance, feeling, "I am in charge here and I won't take any nonsense." Alternatively, one may practice very well within a supportive environment, surrounded by Dharma friends or a spouse who is also a practitioner, but fall apart in the company of others who have no interest in Dharma.

Some of us may find it easy to train our minds with regard to harm from non-human sources, but more difficult where people are concerned. If lightning strikes, if rain comes through the roof, if you stumble and sprain an ankle, there is no culprit to point a finger at. We may be able to integrate a thunderstorm calmly into our practice as we meditate on mental stabilization, but a truck goes rumbling by and we think, "This is terrible! What a lousy retreat facility!" If the wind whistles through the house, there is no problem; but if a person walks by whistling, the thought arises, "Doesn't this guy know that I'm meditating? This is private property. Why can't he be more sensitive when I'm trying to develop bodhicitta?" Our conceptual conditioning is at work here.

Others may have patience for the harm brought on by human beings, but not for animals. We can handle a child's noise, for instance, but a mouse gnawing on tin foil makes us really uptight. An insect bites a person: slap! One sentient being has been mashed. We may feel certain we would never kill a deer or a cat, or even kick a dog. But if there is a rat in the house, out comes the trap.

Or we may draw boundaries arbitrarily in terms of basic ethics. Though we avoid harming human beings physically, we might be less scrupulous about harming them verbally. We might feel quite free to slander people behind their backs, in ways that would seem terrible to their faces. These actions are no less harmful.

These are only a few of the many ways that our practice can

be unbalanced. And practice that is lopsided with bias or prej-
udice does not form a suitable foundation for deep spiritual
growth.

Transform your desires, but remain as you are.

This refers especially to transforming self-centeredness into
cherishing others. If we have been selfish, egocentric, or indifferent to others, these are indeed afflictions of the mind that
should be transformed. But stay the same, the author also says.

Whether we translate the Sanskrit *maitri* and *karuna* as "love"
and "compassion," or understand them in more down-home
terms as "friendliness" and "kindness," these are not essentially outward acts but depend instead on attitude or stance
of mind. How generous we are does not depend on what we
give away, but is a quality of mind. We may have very little
to give away and still be wonderfully generous; we may give
much and be inwardly stingy.

The point is very subtle, as Geshe Rabten brought out when
he discussed this point of practice: Indeed transform your
mind, but make no obvious transformation of your external
behavior or speech. This is not to say that we should leave
all our external behavior unchanged. If our speech tends toward exaggeration, slander, or deviousness, if our physical
habits are clearly unwholesome, we should definitely abandon
such actions. There are many cases when overt wholesome action is appropriate, but the advice here is to be discreet about
it, without calling attention to ourselves.

Why? Because we are gratified when people notice how much
we have changed, it is very easy for our spiritual practice to
become tainted by the eight mundane concerns. Even though
we start out with pure motivation, we may still wind up concerned with our reputation. Will people like us more if we
practice? Will they praise us behind our backs? Will they give
us nice things that we want, or perhaps special advantages?

What gives greater cause for pride than a wholesome transformation of our entire life? This is worth contemplation. We

may be proud of our car, but the car is an external thing. We may be proud of our body, but the body is not really us. It is very easy to feel superior when we see actual transformations in our being. Showing off our virtue to others feeds this, and this should not be where the priority lies.

Many of these practices are concerned with the refinement of actions that are already wholesome. On doing something kind for another person, we have a natural inclination to say, as if waiting for gratitude, "By the way, did you notice how clean your windows are? Did you notice what's in the refrigerator?" The motivation is self-centered and impure. This is not to say that the act is evil; but let's fine-tune it to see if we can simply be satisfied with the act itself, discreetly, instead of looking for a dividend in others' gratification, or expecting a kindness in return. This point—staying where you are while you transform your aspirations—is worthy of serious consideration.

Speak not of degenerate qualities.

Strangely, it is often true that we yearn to speak about the mundane or degenerate characteristics of other people. Perhaps we feel uplifted by observing the faults of others, as if putting others down elevates our own sense of self-worth. Whether someone is untidy, or slothful, or bad at sports, the faults of others seem to place us in a more exalted light.

Within the context of Dharma, this inclination is stimulated as we receive teachings and begin to develop ideals about the transformation of our lives. Conversely, we may see ourselves lacking in terms of these same ideals, and this aggravates dissatisfaction. If we are prone to self-contempt or lack self-love— and I don't mean self-centeredness, but simply an affectionate acceptance of ourselves—this may be exacerbated in the early stages of spiritual practice. As we become more aware of faults, we find more grounds for self-deprecation and disdain, which becomes an uncomfortable burden we carry around like a big bag of rocks. To be rid of even one rock would be a psychological relief.

We may try to unload some weight by directing awareness—our own and others'—away from our own faults. So we pick out the faults of others and talk about them: "Did you notice how Jack fidgets around when he is meditating? He can't sit still. His mind must be a whirlpool of confusion." Perhaps the most odious tendency is to compare ourselves favorably to others: "Did you notice how stingy Joe is? I have my problems too, but I have never acted like that."

Sechibuwa gives the blunt advice, "Don't speak of the mundane faults of others, nor of the faults of their spiritual practice." There may conceivably be very rare occasions when it is appropriate, provided that kindness is the motivation. Even more rarely would it be appropriate to speak of Joe's faults when Joe is not present. But how often when we speak of the faults of others is it really motivated by constructive kindness, by a yearning that the person may be free of this affliction? Perhaps not so often.

Think nothing about the other side.

This next pledge takes the preceding text a step further, moving to an even more subtle level of practice. What does it mean not to think about the other side? We are encouraged here not to dwell mentally on the faults of sentient beings in general, and more specifically, not to dwell upon the faults of those engaging in spiritual practice. Even more specifically, do not dwell on the faults of Dharma friends.

As we enter into spiritual practice and become more sensitive to our own faults, it is probably inevitable that we also become more sensitive to the faults of others. As many of us have experienced, this can be quite an unpleasant phase of practice. We simply seem to be slogging through our own and other people's shortcomings. We set ourselves ideals and we see how we fail to live up to them, and also how other people fail—at least in our own eyes. Now we are being told not to even think of anyone's faults, and particularly not those of

Dharma practitioners and our own companions on the path. It is tremendously refreshing for the mind to simply drop this habit.

When we do observe a fault, what should we do? Regardless of whether we are hunting for faults, they can simply present themselves, as if from the other person's side. An intelligent response is immediately to check the extent to which we are projecting our own faults and past conditioning onto the other person. This is especially effective if we are imputing some mental fault, such as pride, arrogance, or thoughtlessness, upon this person.

How do we know what is in the mind of another person? We judge others' attitudes on the basis of manifest behavior, the verbal and physical expressions evident to us. Unless we are clairvoyant we don't perceive the mind of another person. We may think we know it by the signs that are exhibited, but we are dealing with inference here. Or are we? This question has interesting analogies in many areas of knowledge. In physics, for instance, we never directly perceive the photons, electrons, quarks, and other entities that physicists believe they can infer from manifest phenomena. But if we really investigate the foundations of physics, we find multiple hypotheses to explain the same body of data. The alternative models or presumed entities are limited only by the creativity of our imagination.

So how do we choose which is true among mutually incompatible theories accounting for the same phenomena? Some physicists believe it is a matter of metaphysics. In other words, which one do you like? Where do your metaphysical predilections lie? Which do you find more beautiful? The decision may also be made on pragmatic grounds, e.g., which is easier to work with mathematically? This is not inference; it is simply a matter of choice. The phenomena themselves do not determine which competing theory is correct. As more data is unveiled, the various theories may have to be modified, or perhaps a new one introduced. But there will always be multiple theories. This has been true throughout the history of physics and there is no reason to believe that it will be different in the future.

As in the physical domain, so it is in the mental. Like physics, cognitive psychology tries to infer what is going on in the "black box" of the human mind by imposing conceptual constructs on observed behavior. Rather than looking interoceptively into their own minds, psychologists generally follow the objective ideal that Western science considers to be tried and proven. Adhering to this ideal, they devise models based on *other* people's learning abilities, perception, memory, and other cognitive processes. Nowadays it is fashionable to base an understanding of the human mind on the model of computers. But mutually incompatible theories accounting for the same phenomena, though not much advertised, are as prevalent in cognitive psychology as in physics. Once again we can ask, how do you choose? And the answer is the same: the choice is not determined by the phenomena.

As long as we treat the mind as a black box, we will have mutually incompatible theories of mind accounting for the same phenomena. Consider the case of a person making a gift. Jack gives Mary a small notebook. What do I conclude about Jack? On the one hand, I can think: "It is a very small notebook and Jack is well off; he could at least have given her a larger notebook. Maybe he did not even want it himself, and is getting rid of his trash in the guise of generosity." Or alternatively: "This is a kind and generous act. Jack is considerate and thoughtful." These are just two examples. I could pull another half dozen out of the air to interpret what is going on in Jack's mind. I may even ask him why he gave this notebook to Mary. Whatever he tells me, I then interpret. Was he speaking to me straightforwardly? And so on, endlessly.

When we draw conclusions about other people's minds, this is not inference in any strict, objective sense of the term. We make these judgments on the basis of our experience with other people, but this experience includes no direct perception of their mental processes. The only mental processes that I perceive are my own; and the only context in which I can see the relationship between mental processes and their expressions in speech or action is again exclusively my own.

Thus, my own experience largely determines how I interpret others' actions. If I am a miserly person, I know when I give something that I am expecting at least gratitude if not a more tangible kickback. Likewise, I assume that Jack gives Mary a notebook hoping that she will give him a pen, or that she will take notes for him in class next week. If I simply do not care about my possessions, I assume that Jack also gives the notebook away casually because he doesn't need it. If I am a generous person concerned about the welfare of others, then I see that Mary really needs a notebook and this must be Jack's motivation. Obviously the method is not entirely reliable, because many people are not similar to me.

How can we use this understanding? When another person's fault suddenly becomes glaring, Sechibuwa suggests that we first check whether this might be a fault of our own mind. A fault of our own mind that especially troubles us is likely to be transferred or projected onto others. We see it outside ourselves, instead of inside where it is more painful. It is as if we took a handful of filth and threw it at someone, saying, "Look how dirty you are!" Is the necessary conclusion, therefore, that the other person is pristine pure with no such fault at all? Such teachings sometimes appear in Tibetan Buddhism, but this calls for intelligence. It does not make sense that everyone else is pure and only we are foul.

When we see faults in others, especially mental faults, let us first simply acknowledge that we are making an assumption rather than a necessary inference. It may be accurate, and it may not. Even such ostensibly unwholesome actions as slander, lying, or harming others physically may in fact be appropriate if the motivation is compassion. A parent, for example, may need to punish an unruly child in order to teach a lesson that will prevent the child from coming to grief later on. The word here is caution. Stand back from judgment, and certainly do not dwell on the faults of others. Doing so is a very unpleasant affliction of our own minds.

This applies also to our relationship with a spiritual mentor. The great scriptures of the bodhisattva path encourage us to look upon our teacher as if he or she were a Buddha. Note the precise phrasing, which underlines the difference between this sūtra practice and *tantra:* Look upon the spiritual mentor *as if* he or she were a Buddha. A Buddha has no faults, no obscurations, no distortions, no afflictions. In practice, this means that whenever we see a fault in our spiritual mentor, we should be willing to consider that what we see may actually be a projection of our own mind.

This is why Tibetan lamas encourage us so strongly to be very careful in choosing a spiritual mentor. It is an extremely powerful relationship for transforming our whole being, and not one to rush into casually. It is not easy to be a qualified spiritual teacher of the bodhisattva path. The requirements include deep compassion, deep wisdom, and pure ethics. If we are earnestly following the bodhisattva path, then we are well advised to seek out a truly qualified spiritual mentor, and check this person again and again in a wide variety of circumstances. If we feel that this person is trustworthy and is capable of giving wise and compassionate guidance, then and only then should we enter into this extraordinary relationship.

Keep in mind this most profound point, perhaps in all of Buddhism, that where the teacher is, there is the mind of the Buddha. The awakened consciousness is everywhere pervasive. So, of course, wherever that teacher is, there is the Buddha mind. Our spiritual mentor is as close as we can get for the time being to perceiving the Buddha. I emphasize again that we must be very careful before entering into such a potent relationship. To try out the relationship and then to cripple or abort it has very harmful effects on the student. Better to be cautious. But if we find such a person, then we have indeed found a precious jewel.

To conclude this point, let's return to the issue of how we regard the faults of others—not the spiritual mentor specifically, but simply those around us and especially Dharma friends. If we look with all the clarity and honesty we can muster, and it still seems that another person does indeed have a certain affliction—insensitivity or thoughtlessness, for instance—we conclude that this simply cannot be our projection. Others have noted the same thing. This person really does have a problem. From here we can enter a deeper reality. All faults, whether our own or those of others, should be seen as afflictions, and not as intrinsic elements of that person's being and identity. They are manifesting due to previous causes and conditions, but they are not immutable. Especially if this person is practicing Dharma, we can realistically hope that this distortion will gradually be cleared away. Even if the person is not a Dharma practitioner, we can recognize that like ourselves, he or she is endowed with an essentially pure Buddha nature. The pristine purity of that Buddha nature is veiled adventitiously, and only temporarily, by such mental distortions and obscurations. But they really are not that person's identity.

To realize this is a tremendous boon requiring continual practice, and we should apply it to ourselves as well as others. When we start to belittle ourselves for our own faults, recognize that they are simply afflictions obscuring our own essential purity and our capacity for full awakening. These temporary distortions are not who we are, and we do have the means for overcoming them. This is what Buddhadharma is all about: the dispelling of distortions and obscurations. If we can develop a sympathy and gentleness towards ourselves—not complacency but self-love in the best sense of the term—then, when we see faults in others we can transfer to them the wisdom we have acquired internally. Even if a fault seems quite blatant, instead of responding with agitation and intolerance, we can recognize it sympathetically as an affliction similar to those we suffer ourselves. Rather than disparaging the sufferer, the yearning can then easily arise out of kindness: "May that person be free of this fault, which so evidently brings unhappiness to them and to those around them."

Abandon all hope for results.

We can dispense first with some very mundane hopes that are not worth nurturing at all: the hope, for example, that others might esteem us more highly as a result of our practice, or offer us service or devotion. Geshe Chekawa identifies other hopes that should not be cultivated: the hope of being invulnerable to harm, or the self-centered hope of attaining a fortunate rebirth, or liberation, or even Buddhahood, as a result of practice. Most important, we are encouraged not to cultivate hopes for great or swift benefits as the result of practice.

There is a natural tendency, when our practice starts to go well, to get excited at the prospect of attaining wonderful results very quickly. This excitement is believed to attract *māras*, malignant entities who create obstacles for us. It is like turning on a neon sign in our thoughts that says, "I am on the verge of a great breakthrough! Hey māras, come and get it!" Avoid this, because experience teaches us that this kind of excitement over hopes of great and swift results, rather than enhancing the practice, simply creates problems in our meditation.

The question of hope and anxiety is important in spiritual practice, especially when we enter into sustained and earnest meditative practice. Meditative quiescence is a prime example. The treatises of the great contemplatives describe in detail the benefits of this practice and how to cultivate it; upon its attainment, how readily one can develop clairvoyance and other psychic powers; and the tremendously wholesome qualities of consciousness that result—the physical and mental bliss, the serenity, the stability, and the transcendence of mundane experience. Tsongkhapa and others have described these benefits to kindle our incentive for practicing earnestly and with perseverance. What is likely to result, of course, is the hope of attaining meditative quiescence. Moreover, if we are dealing with a limited time span, as we all are, we naturally hope to attain it in a year, or three months... "And then I can go on and develop bodhicitta in three months and realization of emptiness in another three months, and then tantra and...." Not that it is impossible, but beating this drum primes us for anxiety, especially when we bracket our hopes in terms of a specific time, a specific place, and a specific technique. We set up a situation of subtle, internal panic as we wonder unconsciously, "Am I on schedule? Will I meet the deadline?" Whether or not we believe in external māras, we certainly have these māras of mental affliction within our own minds.

In the beginning stages of a practice, self-centeredness is a useful incentive. Instead of simply abandoning it, we gradually strain it out. As Śāntideva says in his *Guide to a Bodhisattva's Way of Life*, if you don't think of developing bodhicitta for your own sake, how can you ever aspire to develop it for others? And his first chapter is devoted exclusively to the benefits of developing bodhicitta. Whether the practice is Mind Training, meditative quiescence, bodhicitta, or the realization of emptiness, an awareness of the benefits as well as the potential problems and their antidotes provides us with a clear understanding of how to engage correctly in the practice. The results will come from correct practice done with earnestness, a proper level of intensity, and continuity over a long period of time. They will not come faster by anticipating or longing for them.

Abandon poisonous food.

The next verse does not refer to dietary restrictions, but is a continuation of the same theme. Engaging in spiritual practice is very much like eating. The whole point of eating is to benefit ourselves: to nourish the body, to gain strength and vitality, and to rid ourselves of hunger pangs. Poisonous food defeats the purpose of eating.

As we engage in spiritual practice, we pollute our spiritual food with poison by remaining unaware of self-grasping and the egotism and self-centeredness that derive from it. If we do not discard these as enemies that afflict us but instead simply accept them, our practice is like eating poisoned food. There is no question that one can meditate assiduously, translate books and become a great scholar, or even an articulate teacher, and still have self-centeredness at the very core of one's involvement in Dharma. Whether our practice is as profound as Kālacakra, Mahāmudrā, or Dzogchen, or as straightforward as breath awareness and loving kindness, if we approach it with a mind that is grasping onto the inherent existence of phenomena, it acts as cause for further cycling in saṃsāra. We may be trying to do something of benefit, but self-grasping pollutes the spiritual practice like a poison. It acts as a cause of further suffering and therefore should be abandoned.

Do not devote yourself kindly to the central object.

This pledge also seems obscure at first. The Tibetan word translated here as *central object* refers to a central pillar or support, and is interpreted here as our own mental distortions. In other words, we should not bear a gentle, lenient attitude towards our own mental distortions. If we find ourselves responding with resentment to another person's disagreeable or unkind action, we should not treat our own distortion casually, saying, "What's a little bit of hostility or arrogance now and then?" This genial attitude to our own afflictions is to be abandoned, because it nurtures the distortion and prolongs it for days, years, and even decades, causing suffering for ourselves and others.

Do not laugh at malicious jokes.

The commentary here says more than the verse itself: Do not make bad jokes. The author is not advising us to avoid bad puns, but is referring to malicious sarcasm. Don't make fun of other people in ways that would bring pain to their hearts. The temptation is especially strong when it entails the double satisfaction of disparaging another person and exalting ourselves at the same time by showing off our cleverness. Those of us prone to this type of humor need to address this by changing the conditioning of our speech. All types of harsh speech should be abandoned to avoid harming ourselves and others as well.

Do not wait at the narrow passageway.

Picture a scene from a western, or from the highlands of Tibet: bandits waiting in ambush at a narrow pass, where the victim has no chance of escape. To really damage someone, one waits till one's intended victim is most vulnerable. What we are told to avoid here is biding our time to be especially hurtful, lashing back at someone maybe weeks or months after they have injured us, whether physically or verbally.

On first hearing verses such as this we may assume they do not apply to us. Obviously, this is meant for malicious people, and we are not among the bad guys. Perhaps this initial response is honest; some of us may hold no grudges. If so, we need not be concerned with this right now; we have certainly practiced well in the past, either in this or previous lifetimes. Let us focus instead on problems that are relevant.

But our initial response may not be very insightful. In meditating on this pledge as well as the others, the point is to examine our past experience and try to recall: Have I done this kind of thing before? What was the context? What prodded me to do it? What were the results? Do I still have this tendency? And in the present, any resentment still active should be brought to light. Am I anticipating revenge? There are ways of getting back at others more subtle than standing at the ready with a shotgun. We need to check for ourselves whether each pledge is pertinent for our present situation, but they are all worthy of clear-minded, honest introspection that does not rely on the initial response, "Who, me?" Maybe, after more reflection, we may say, "Well, yes, at times." This does not mean that we are evil and vulgar, but simply that we have some work to do.

Do not load the burden of a dzo on an ox.

A *dzo* is a cross between an ox and a yak—a very strong beast of burden. So the message is: don't take the burden of a dzo and place it upon an ox, which is a weaker animal. This rustic metaphor refers to issues of ability and responsibility. Each of us is endowed with certain talents, whether we were born with them or earned them in this life. We also have our responsibilities, some of which we may not be inclined to fulfill. If this text were originally written in America, it would probably say here: Don't pass the buck. Recognize what your role is and what you are here to contribute. What are your special abilities and responsibilities? At times these will be enjoyable and rewarding; at other times they may be grunt work. But having identified the grunt work, don't shift it onto other people's shoulders. They may not be as capable as you are for the task.

Do not direct yourself to the summit of the ascent.

This next verse is difficult to understand as the words are not clear, and various possible spellings for the text change the meaning radically. However we translate the text, the commentary remains straightforward. When you are working with other people, sharing in any kind of project, don't stand up to claim credit for the work. In other words, don't seek out the limelight. This needs no further elaboration.

Some of these precepts are bound to be more useful than others, but it is worthwhile giving each of them a chance. Examine whether we tend to seek out the limelight, to pass the buck, to be sarcastic, and so forth. Such tendencies as we have, we can counteract, and this will be to our own benefit. The purpose of the training is not to set down laws and regulations, but simply to derive benefit.

Do not be devious.

This is also very straightforward. The commentary gives as an example the pretense that you are accepting a loss from someone else while in fact you stand to benefit. Again, not much elaboration is needed. Being devious, cunning, or sly has no place in a life that is oriented towards Dharma.

Do not let the gods descend to the devil.

The commentary speaks first of devas, gods like those of the Hindu or Greek pantheons. Many accounts suggest that these non-human beings can be rather fickle. If you honor and worship them, they may help you. If you don't, they may turn around and injure you, in which case the god descends to a devil, an inflictor of harm.

What does it really mean for the divine to descend to the diabolical? The point of the Mind Training is to subdue our own mind: to gradually vanquish self-grasping and the mental afflictions that arise from it. No matter how intensely, earnestly, and diligently we practice, we may still inflate ourselves with a sense of superiority, using our spiritual practice as an unfortunate source of conceit. This distortion of the practice is the descent from a deva to a demon, from a god to a devil.

The commentary offers a wonderful analogy here. You are standing guard, vigilant at the front door of your house, while a thief climbs in the back window and robs you blind. As diligent as your efforts are, they are working against you, simply because your attitude towards the practice is misconstrued. The profundity of any practice is a function not only of the technique but also of the practitioner. A human being cannot be fundamentally superficial, because the Buddha nature we each have is an utterly pure and divine essence; but a person who is trite and dilettantish in terms of conscious behavior can trivialize an ostensibly profound practice. The corollary is also true, that a profound person cannot practice superficially.

On hearing teachings that are said to be rare and secret and

only for the most advanced practitioners, we may feel that we
have managed to slip through the door of an elite club. We
can fool ourselves that the visualization or mantra or whatever practice we have learned is extremely profound; but that
may not be true for us right now. Sometimes the most profound thing we can do is to meditate simply on the continuity
of consciousness from lifetime to lifetime, the fact that different sequential lives are related by our actions, and that right
now we are creating our future even as we experience the results
of our past actions. Something as straightforward as this is a
profound practice when contemplated by a profound mind.
But even the most advanced tantric techniques are not profound if we come to them with a superficial mind.

Why do we engage in any spiritual practice? The answer that
Buddhism emphasizes is our own vulnerability to suffering,
whether blatant or as an undercurrent of anxiety. If we are
deeply aware that we need help and recognize that without
Dharma our minds are dysfunctionally creating misery, it becomes ridiculous to hold a supercilious attitude. It is hard to
be pompous when the reason for practicing is a desire to be
free of our own mental distortions. The Four Noble Truths—
the existence of suffering, the source of suffering, freedom from
suffering and its source, and the means of achieving such
freedom—are very sobering in this regard.

Do not seek another's misery as a way to your own happiness.

This final precept may be pertinent for many of us. The commentator provides several examples, one of which concerns in-
heritance. Anticipating the death of a relative or rich friend
in hopes of benefiting is certainly a case of seeking another's
misery for the sake of your own happiness. Another major example concerns people whom we cannot stand. We may be
gladdened at the prospect of an enemy dying, or falling into
disgrace, or getting hit by a truck. Our imagination can become very fertile here, but such thoughts are to be abandoned.

Sechibuwa also gives as example a meditator or Dharma

teacher vying for reputation with others in the same region, thinking that the illness or death of a peer would result in greater respect or more offerings for oneself. This brings to mind contemporary examples from business or academia, where people compete for their own happiness to the detriment of their colleagues. The arena of sex provides other examples: breaking up a harmonious relationship because of lust for one of the people involved. The envy and selfishness of such actions are tragic.

Whether an enemy meets with misfortune, sickness, or death, is a matter of his or her own karma. Our own history and past actions determine the fortune or misfortune presented to each of us. Wishing misfortune on someone does not cause that misfortune to happen. Instead, because the yearning for another person's suffering is itself an unwholesome mental action, it immediately places unwholesome imprints upon our own mind and guarantees our own future suffering if those imprints are not purified.

The Seventh Point
The Practices of Mind Training

The seventh and final point concerns the practices, or disciplines, of the Mind Training. As Sechibuwa comments, these are means for preventing our spiritual maturity from degenerating and for encouraging its further increase. Like the pledges of the sixth point, this entails a series of many parts, applicable to many occasions and facets of life. As with the pledges, it is worthwhile to look at just a few each day. Don't attempt all twenty at once or they may overload you. Meditate quietly on a few of them for a short time, and then hold them in mind throughout the day. The great advantage of the Mind Training is that it does not matter how busy we are. For those who yearn to practice Dharma in a very active life, the Mind Training presents an opportunity and material to work with. But it does require some time, perhaps just ten or twenty minutes daily, to recall instances from the past that relate to the point at hand; instances, for example, when we may indeed have sought out our own happiness at the expense of others. Recollect that we are not immune to the faults in question, and then, having looked to the past, anticipate how these faults might surface today in subtle ways or gross.

There are certain forms of behavior that are incompatible with living happily in this life, and that damage the possibility of a fortunate rebirth in the future. Moreover, on a deep level of practice, such behavior is counter-productive inasmuch as we are seeking to cultivate meditative quiescence, loving kindness, compassion, or realization of the ultimate nature of reality. It is as if we were setting off on a long sea voyage while, for a hobby, whacking a hole into our ship with a pickaxe— not a very good way to stay afloat. Avoiding such action is the purpose of precepts in general, whether monastic or bodhisattva precepts, and also of these prescriptions for practice. No one is going to police us, nor are we taking these as formal precepts, but insofar as we recognize unwholesome patterns that are incompatible with our deepest yearning for a meaningful life, it is to our advantage to strain them out and replace them with a new type of conditioning. Familiarizing ourselves with wholesome patterns of behavior so that they become spontaneous is indeed a conditioning. Some of these practices will not be spontaneous at first, because transforming ingrained patterns of behavior can require arduous effort.

Given that some of our ingrained patterns of behavior are unwholesome, there are obviously occasions when it is improper for us to be spontaneous and natural. But as we recognize these and restructure our behavior, then more and more of our spontaneous responses become wholesome ones, and we can increasingly trust our natural, effortless behavior. Then we can allow the spontaneity to express itself freely with a high degree of inner trust. The culmination of this process is full Buddhahood, in that all of the actions of the Buddha are spontaneous, unpremeditated, and perfectly effortless. This is certainly a direction worth striving towards, and we can create facsimiles of the goal, moment by moment, in our present daily life.

Practice all yogas by means of one.

Thousands upon thousands of practices are presented within the context of Buddhism. Aside from the practices intended while sitting cross-legged in meditation, there are specific practices for eating, sleeping, and manifold situations, each with individual actions. But Sechibuwa points out that those of us who have entered the door of this Dharma can practice the essence of all those yogas, or spiritual practices, by means of the Mind Training. This training, which essentially is the cultivation of the two bodhicittas, can transform any other type of activity, particularly for those of us leading very active lives where the demands of the practice may struggle against the demands that life circumstances make on our time. This tension between the longing for more time for spiritual practice, and the needs of family, job, and bills to pay, is not necessarily a negative thing. What we do with it is the critical point.

One possible response is to conclude that spiritual growth is the very core of the meaning of human existence and everything else takes a back seat to it. In this case we forget the struggle and devote our life to spiritual practice, even at the sacrifice of things that would otherwise lie within grasp, such as wealth, fame, reputation, and luxury. Another response assumes spiritual practice to be impractically difficult and unrealistic, in which case we leave it to others, or maybe for later when we have more time, perhaps after retirement. We focus on more important things like making money to pay the bills, and the spiritual practice is pushed into the background, at zero magnitude or just minimum maintenance.

Consider a third possible response. As adults living in contemporary society with obligations to others such as our children, we recognize that it would be irresponsible to walk out, regardless of how much we are drawn to the spiritual life. It is simply not appropriate. Remember the Buddha's life in this context. If you are confident that you will attain enlightenment within a short period as the Buddha did, then I would recommend that you walk out today. The Buddha was able to return with such blessings for his family that the grief they felt on his leaving was outshone, as the stars are outshone by the sun when it rises in the morning. If you have that confidence, then even the needs of a family must be abandoned.

But unless you have that confidence, their demands on your time are legitimate.

So, recognizing that we have certain obligations, and recognizing at the same time that spiritual practice is the core of a meaningful life, what do we do? There really is an answer. It is not easy, but it is tremendously fruitful, and it keeps on opening and opening further: transform those actions that are already obligations by applying Dharma to them.

Take eating, for instance. We have to do it two or three times a day, but we don't have to wolf down the food. There is no one who cannot sit and pause first for thirty seconds. Even fast-food is worth the thirty seconds it takes to recognize the immense number of beings who have provided us with this food. Pausing like this ties us into the community of life, at least on planet earth, as we recognize that we are indebted to others. We have received, and as we take the food, let us do it with the aspiration, "May this be returned. May I use my abilities to the fullest to serve those who have served me." And that includes everyone, directly or indirectly. The service may occur on a very mundane level, but insofar as we mature spiritually, our responsibility increases according to our abilities. Not because someone tells us, "Now you have to do this," but simply as we gain insight into the nature and sources of suffering and of contentment, then we have something all the more valuable to offer others.

Eating, taking care of the body, going on vacations, can all be a part of spiritual practice. All of us need time to relax, but it need not be a break in spiritual practice if we recognize this too as a way to refresh ourselves, restoring vitality, good cheer, and balance so that we can serve again with creativity and intelligence.

With this one yoga we can transform everything we do. All of our actions can be employed in the cultivation of ultimate and relative bodhicitta. For those of us with many demands on our time, this is an utterly priceless system of practice. It can ease the tension between the mundane demands of the world and those of the spirit by transforming worldly activity into a source of spiritual nourishment for ourselves and others.

Counteract all withdrawal by means of one.

The root text for the second practice instructs us to use one attitude to counteract all withdrawal. Entering into a spiritual practice, we may occasionally come to the morose conclusion that we were better off before we started. We may feel that our own mental distortions are stronger, that we are more up-tight, or that people seem to get angry at us more often. Perhaps our family disapproves of our practicing Buddhism. We may feel that the emphasis on service in the cultivation of bodhicitta demands a kind of spiritual suicide: giving up everything, never thinking of ourselves. We become dejected and withdraw, thinking that the project ahead of us is hopelessly overwhelming: there is just so much housecleaning to do in this mind of ours. Procrastination becomes a wonderful crutch here. Maybe when we are older, or better yet in the next lifetime, then it will be easier. We put our practice in the back seat or throw it out the window altogether. What to do?

First of all, when we become discouraged and begin to withdraw, recognize what is happening: "I am disillusioned with the practice. I thought I would progress more quickly than I have." Then recognize also that in this world there are so many, many beings who, like ourselves, are striving for happiness and wishing to be free of suffering, and who are engaging in ineffective means for accomplishing these ends. Sechibuwa suggests that we counteract dejection by reaching out to all sentient beings around us. Offer them our body, our virtues, and our prayers that they may meet with effective means for finding true happiness and freeing themselves of suffering.

There are two actions on two occasions, at the beginning and end.

The third of the practices listed here is one very frequently quoted by Tibetan lamas, and extremely important. The beginning occasion for each day is getting up in the morning. What is our first thought on waking up? We can all afford a couple of minutes in bed to prepare quietly for the day before jumping up and brushing our teeth. Sechibuwa suggests that an earnest practitioner of the Mind Training should at this point be setting motivation, resolving not be polluted by self-centeredness for the course of the day. It is important to understand exactly what is meant by self-centeredness, so that it is clearly demarcated when it arises in the mind during the day: "I recognize this; I was looking at something similar just this morning." And then the teaching of the Mind Training can come flooding in.

Again, don't be lenient with self-centeredness. Recognize this quality of mind that has brought us misery, discontent, anxiety, and frustration, year after every year of this lifetime, not to speak of lifetimes before this since time out of mind. Each morning, look at the day that is yet to unfold and really set up the aspiration not to succumb to the self-centeredness, not to value our own welfare as the priority in our daily activities. This is a perfectly feasible transformation of the mind. Anticipate responding to others with concern and sensitivity for their well-being, go into the day with this stance, and then be aware and introspectively alert in dealing with people during the day. Be aware of the quality of your mind as you work, drive, shop, take care of the children, watch TV. In other words, having set the resolve, carry through; not because the karmic results will injure us if we don't, but because we yearn to live a meaningful and contented life that opens up to greater and greater happiness for ourselves and others. Cherish that thought and motivation throughout the course of the day.

If we cannot cultivate introspective alertness, even during our busiest days, then we might as well discard that way of life, because it is guaranteed to be meaningless. Get rid of it and do something different. Obviously, I am not recommending suicide, but a change of lifestyle. Our children, spouse, and friends are not benefiting from it, and we certainly are not ourselves. What are we actually offering to our children in such a situation? The most emphatic lesson that children learn is not the words we say, but the substantial example that we demonstrate in the quality of our life. Those of us who claim to have no time for any kind of Dharma practice, whether teachings, meditation, or transforming daily actions into Dharma, have set for our children the poorest possible example; and unless they rebel, they will waste their own lives as we have encouraged them.

Employment in service, as a nurse, teacher, doctor, or monk, may sometimes substitute for living a truly meaningful life. There is still a karmic benefit: healing others is wholesome. But if the motivation is chiefly to earn a good living, the benefits are limited. We may enjoy the fruit of good health in a future life, for example, or meet with skilled doctors when we are sick ourselves, but meanwhile we remain mentally imbalanced and miserable. There is no substitute for internal spiritual practice.

At the end of the day, when we lie down ready to sleep, then again it is worth taking at least a few moments to look back and examine the events of the day. Remember the original resolve and recognize the occasions when self-centeredness and mental distortions arose and dominated our thoughts and perhaps our physical actions. Guilt has no place in this recognition. (Interestingly, *guilt* has no translation in Tibetan, although *remorse* does.) Simply recognize that we have engaged in actions motivated by self-centeredness that bring us harm, squandering the wonderful potential of this human life, damaging ourselves and others. And with that recognition, recall how to counteract the self-centeredness and mental distortion. There is no way to snap our fingers and be free of such unwholesome behavior, but we do know the antidotes. So look to the future and say, "This is something to avoid, for everyone's welfare."

This is not simply a matter of scrutinizing the unwholesome events like a judge. Recognize also the victories, the delights of implementing the spiritual practice, and the times when we acted with real cherishing of others. Look back and rejoice at the acts of service that were not calculated to elicit a reward or even gratitude. These acts are answers to the question of how we can make life meaningful. Recognize occasions of insight, when we have seen ourselves or others without the reification of an autonomous, intrinsic identity. Rejoice in this cultivation of wisdom, because this also is a way to make life meaningful.

Other commentaries on this verse frequently refer to cultivating the motivation before beginning any endeavor: "May this act as a cause for my full awakening for the benefit of all creatures." In other words, allow the relative bodhicitta to enter and provide the incentive for engaging in that endeavor, which tremendously enriches it. Then, at the conclusion of a wholesome action, or at the end of the day, look back and once again dedicate its merit to full awakening for the benefit of all beings, and to anything else that seems of great worth, such as peace on this planet. We can offer this merit, or spiritual power, and we can keep on offering it: the more we offer, the more we have.

Whichever of the opposites occurs, be patient.

The polarities referred to in this fourth practice are good fortune and misfortune. When we meet with good fortune, we tend to respond with attachment to the situation. Getting a raise or a promotion, being praised or coming into wealth, all commonly produce a sense of self-inflation. A more beneficial response to good fortune is not allowing our mind to come under the domination of the eight worldly concerns of momentary pleasure and pain, gain and loss, praise and blame, good and bad reputation.

The point is to respond with a greater sense of inner stability and equanimity. Of course, we enjoy the good fortune. Being a Buddhist does not require being a spoil-sport with a glum face. But avoiding attachment, conceit, or a sense of superiority does require patience in the face of good fortune. *Patience* in this context sounds odd in English, but it entails the same clarity and calmness of mind that helps us to avoid getting flustered in the face of adversity.

Likewise for the opposite polarity. It is easy when we meet with misfortune, poverty, loss of reputation or status in our job, or a calamity such as the loss of a loved one, to lose enthusiasm for Dharma in the depths of our disillusionment. But instead of succumbing to despair in the face of adversity, seek to cultivate that inner strength which is really what patience is about: inner courage as ballast for your vessel of life.

Related to this is the tendency to judge our Dharma practice superficially, on the basis of external circumstances. When life is treating us well, we feel that Dharma is good. We might give it half an hour every day religiously, and think that the job is done because the rest of our waking day is going well. A Dharma practitioner should view the pleasures of a good job, a healthy family situation, comfortable living circumstances, and a sound economy, with suitable delight, as we would look at a very pleasant painting balanced upon a structure of match sticks. This is happiness due to pleasant external stimuli, which by and large are beyond our control. A Buddhist response is not in any way to begrudge these mundane pleasures, but at the same time not to use them as a substitute for Dharma practice. This is not so obvious during the good times, but it becomes very apparent maybe a little too late, during the bad times.

Guard the two at the cost of your life.

The "two" referred to here are, first, any precepts we have taken on ourselves in general in our Dharma practice, and second, the specific pledges, precepts, and practices of this Mind Training. Guard these, Geshe Chekawa says, even at the cost of our life. This is a demanding statement, and very earnestly meant. There are some things more precious than one's life. Several lamas have commented to me that there is no value in a long life if it is dominated by unwholesome actions of body, speech, and mind. Obviously, in such a life one is simply polluting one's stream of consciousness, sowing seeds year after year for the repercussions of further suffering and misery. What is it that brings value and benefit to the very core of a life? It is our Dharma practice. Rather than sacrifice our spiritual practice, it is better to sacrifice a life.

Practice the three austerities.

Austerity refers to something difficult and arduous. What are these three things that are so difficult to do? The first is bearing in mind the antidotes to mental distortions; the second is turning away from the mental distortions; the third is cutting their continuum.

The first austerity is simply to be aware from hour to hour, from moment to moment, of the quality of thoughts that arise in our mind. It is pleasant to savor a mind that is relatively undistorted, with a sense of balance that does not hinge upon external stimuli or even on sucking the conceptual thumb of a pleasant thought. As you become aware, you can ascertain these wholesome states of mind, despite the subtle currents of self-grasping that remain.

Then, when this wholesome state becomes distorted, try to remain aware. This takes some practice. The mental distortions that arise may shape themselves as anger or resentment dwelling on some abuse or thoughtlessness received, or as anxiety focused on attachment. Whatever form they take, they disrupt the internal harmony of the mind, its poise and clarity. Recognizing these mental distortions as they arise, recollect their antidotes.

Some antidotes work like a scatter gun, effective against many distortions. Relative bodhicitta is a great fire that burns up all kinds of mental distortions, and insight into emptiness is likewise a blast furnace that incinerates them all. But until we are truly adept at cultivating the two bodhicittas, relative and ultimate, there are many other antidotes within reach. Śāntideva, especially in the sixth chapter of his *Guide to the Bodhisattva's Way of Life*, offers a whole repertoire of very accessible practices. We need not be saints or profound contemplatives to practice these effective antidotes for specific mental distortions, although they can be difficult.

The easiest thing to do when a mental distortion arises is to ride with it like a hitchhiker. We are sticking our thumb out in a neutral or wholesome state of mind, and then some guy comes along in a black vehicle of mental distortions, picks us up and carries us away. When a mental distortion arises, we naturally identify with it and go with it. The mind is not aware of the mental distortion but is focused instead on the subject of the distortion: the enemy or the thing we are grasping after. This is the conditioning we have to overcome.

The second austerity, after awareness of the antidotes, is to turn away from the mental distortion. Point a finger and say, "Alright anger, resentment, attachment, jealousy, I see you. I know what you are doing to me and I am not going along for the ride. Your time is up." It may be a crude response, but it is better than riding with it as a passive victim. Recognize the distortion, recall the specific antidote, apply the antidote, and pull out. Like a jet going into a nose dive, it may be hard to pull against the momentum, but with effort it can be done.

The third austerity is cutting the continuum of the mental distortions. This is the hardest of all, but we can start by cultivating a resolve, once we have recognized the mental distortion and turned away from it, not to succumb to this kind of distortion in the future. The final antidote, of course, is direct realization of the nature of ultimate truth. From a Buddhist perspective this is the only effective means for ultimately cutting the mental distortions forever, so that they can never afflict us again. The misconstruing of reality through confusion and ignorance lies at the very root of all other mental distortions. To cut that root we need to saturate the mind with the experience, and not simply the concept, of the nature of ultimate reality.

Acquire the three principal causes.

The three principal causes here refer to the causes leading to spiritual growth or awakening. The first cause is developing a relationship with a spiritual mentor who is well trained in practical guidance through a lineage of teachers, and is also endowed with insight.

I would add to the commentary that it is very important for Dharma practitioners, not least those who are teachers, to be endowed with sound learning. We need not become erudite scholars, but we should have a clear understanding of the practices we engage in. And for acquiring a sound theoretical knowledge, there is no substitute for a teacher. Books alone can never be a substitute; to come to life they must be moistened with the oral teachings of a competent teacher. Learning by itself is barren, and also terribly hard, without experience and insight. If either of these is missing, then the learning is likely to compound our mental distortions with a sense of arrogant superiority. This is known as spiritual pride, and it is a dangerous pitfall if we are simply acquiring more and more knowledge without putting it into practice.

There is also a danger in focusing only on the practice, as if philosophy and theory were just for scholars and the real essence lay in a certain set of spiritual techniques. One can be a stupid yogi no less than a barren scholar.

There is no rule that we must complement our practice with theoretical knowledge, but it helps avoid pitfalls. For instance, a knowledge of the stages of insight beyond our present state will prevent us from blowing out of proportion such realization as we have gained. Otherwise, for example, it is tempting to think we have achieved meditative quiescence as soon as we have accomplished a little bit of mental stabilization, or that we have become bodhisattvas as soon as we have developed a little kindness.

The most prevalent pitfall is misjudgment concerning insight. Someone meditates, or watches a sunset, or maybe takes psychedelic drugs, and assumes they have realized emptiness or *dharmakāya*. Years ago, a Westerner with very little training in Dharma and apparently very little practice came to Geshe Rabten, who had just become abbot of the monastery at Rikon in Switzerland. The fellow informed Geshe Rabten that he had attained *sambhogakāya*, the extremely subtle body of a Buddha, and he asked what to do next. He commented that he was perturbed by the awareness that he had very little compassion. Geshe Rabten felt that there was nothing he could do for someone so fixed on the absurd notion of his own state of realization, so he responded, "Well, why don't you go out the front door of the monastery and take a right."

This emphasizes the critical need for both sound theoretical understanding and practical engagement. And as much as we need these ourselves, they are indispensable prerequisites for an authentic spiritual guide.

We can save a lot of time and unnecessary suffering by seeking out the first of the three principal causes, a qualified spiritual mentor. But no guru is a substitute for our own intuitive wisdom. Each of us is endowed with the innate potential for insight that is our Buddha nature, and the external teacher is there to unveil this intuitive wisdom. Keep in mind also that many people who claim to be spiritual teachers or enlightened gurus are unqualified from the Buddhist perspective. Simply be very cautious; we can derive far more benefit by patiently seeking out someone who has true depth and substance.

The second principal cause is devoting ourselves to realization: applying ourselves to gaining realization of such truths expressed in Buddhism as the preciousness of human life, right up to the realization of ultimate truth. Regardless of the quality of our spiritual mentor or the amount of learning we have acquired, none of this will transform our lives unless we apply ourselves to earnest practice.

The third principal cause entails creating favorable circumstances for our Dharma practice. Some of these are internal, such as faith, intelligence, and enthusiasm. Each of these internal conditions necessary for a beneficial practice is malleable. We are not simply given a fixed amount of intelligence, for example. Intelligence is flexible. It diminishes if not used or if used in a stupid fashion, and it can also be enhanced. The monastic universities of Tibet spent two to three years training the students' intelligence before applying the intelligence to such things as the Perfection of Wisdom teachings, logic, epistemology, ontology, ethics, phenomenology, and so forth. Like intelligence, faith certainly is a prerequisite for any kind of major endeavour, whether in business, philosophy, science, or Dharma. If you don't have faith in what you are doing, you're not going to get anywhere. The same is true of enthusiasm. In addition to these necessary internal conditions for a fruitful Dharma practice, there are, of course, the external situations. Without sufficient food, clothing, and shelter, for example, we cannot proceed.

If, on reviewing our present situation, we find that we are already endowed with the three principal causes, then rejoice. If we do not have the three, then we should certainly seek to acquire them. But in the meantime we can again transform the unfavorable situation, as we have done before, by recollecting how so many sentient beings are also bereft of these three principal causes. Cultivate compassion for them by taking their misfortune into your heart. Practice the taking and the sending, offering your own merit with the prayer: "May each sentient being be endowed with the necessary causes for his or her spiritual growth and happiness."

Cultivate the absence of three degenerations.

This concerns the three elements of spiritual practice that can degenerate, and how to prevent them from doing so.

The first is the faith in one's spiritual mentor. Sechibuwa writes that all virtue on the Mahāyāna path depends on such faith and reverence. In the bodhisattva aspect of the practice, this is achieved by looking upon the spiritual mentor as if he or she were a fully awakened Buddha. The purpose of this reverence is a quality of awareness that is extremely fertile for wholesome change, realization, and enthusiasm. Some texts even say that faith is the mother of all realizations.

The second element is not allowing our enthusiasm for the Mind Training to wane. Enthusiasm is indispensable to a fruitful spiritual practice. If the practice simply becomes a grind that we perform out of a sense of responsibility, it is not likely to last long or produce much good fruit.

The third element is not allowing our sense of conscience with respect to these practices to degenerate. Conscience here implies an inwardly directed alertness. If I do something in the privacy of my own room that is incompatible with Dharma, I feel it. Insofar as we can maintain this quality of awareness when we engage in inappropriate actions of body, speech, or mind, this inner attentiveness responds quickly, saying, "This is an indulgence I don't want to pursue."

The counterpart to conscience is regard for others. If we demonstrate some crude behavior in the company of others, then our awareness steps in to remind us that this is not how we want to demonstrate our life to the world; this behavior is incompatible with our ideals. Although the awareness is publicly oriented, the bottom line is our own principles. Do not confuse this with getting hung up on what other people think. If I spend time in meditation, will they think I am a flake? If I pick up a caterpillar off the sidewalk and put it in a safe place, will they think I am strange? Such consideration for the opinion of others is misguided because in fact these actions are wholesome.

Be endowed with the three inseparables.

The inseparables are three things from which we should not be separated: spiritual practice in body, speech, and mind. As examples of spiritual practice in body, the text mentions service to one's spiritual mentor, offerings to the Triple Gem, and devotional practices such as circumambulation around sacred reliquaries. We can elaborate on these to include any type of physical service or wholesome action that is chiefly of the body.

Verbal spiritual practice consists of reciting the verses of taking refuge or praying for the benefit of the world, and includes
any type of wholesome speech. A word of kindness is verbal
spiritual action. Thirdly, spiritual practice of the mind focuses
especially on the cultivation of relative and ultimate bodhicitta.

It is important to understand the meaning of spiritual practice broadly, and not confine it to sitting cross-legged in meditation, or reciting verses, or doing prostrations. In an active
working life, it is truly possible to have our spiritual practice
permeate many activities that would otherwise be totally mundane. The crucial point here is the wholesome motivation for
these actions. If during daily life we maintain an attentiveness
to the practices we have adopted, this itself becomes spiritual
practice.

It is important also not to ritualize our practice too much.
Formality sets up an unnecessary dichotomy between spiritual
practice and daily life. Guilt is unnecessary, and there is no
need for internal conflict between Dharma practice and the
enjoyment of having friends over for an evening, going for a
vacation, or a walk in the park. By telling ourselves, "If I were
really a Dharma practitioner, I would not go skiing," we set
up internal strife. It is far more fruitful to integrate our spiritual
practice with our daily life. Eventually, through the natural
process of transforming our minds, we may find ourselves less
inclined to turn for our enjoyment to areas that most people
find necessary, or at least attractive. Allowing this process to
unfold naturally avoids a lot of unnecessary painful struggle.

Always meditate on those who make you boil.

The text of the tenth practice is obscure. In trying to make
sense of the Tibetan, I remember a comment Geshe Ngawang
Dhargyey made while teaching a classical text by Atīśa. He
said that a very learned lama would be able to give ten or fif-
teen justifiable interpretations of the same text, depending on
the person whom he was teaching. It is helpful to keep in mind
that there may not be just one meaning intended here; the

challenge for practitioners, including teachers, is to draw as much meaning from it as possible.

One interpretation, suggested in the commentary and very rich in meaning, is continually to meditate on people with whom we come into frequent and intimate contact. We tend to let our Dharma practice slide a bit with people we see constantly, whereas we practice much more earnestly with strangers or in other contexts. Sechibuwa encourages us here to pay special attention to people who may be resentful towards us. The work place provides clear examples, where people we meet all the time may be competing with us in the eyes of our employer. Hold these people especially in mind in the context of practice.

Sechibuwa provides three other examples in a different vein: our spiritual mentor, our parents, and bodhisattvas. Concerning beings such as these, he says, any evil we do them has very severe karmic results. For this reason, we owe a special conscientiousness toward these beings.

Do not rely on other conditions.

The eleventh practice is especially rich. The commentator points out that we may need very specific conditions or external circumstances for other Dharma practices. A paradigmatic example is the cultivation of meditative quiescence. Living in downtown New York, in an apartment full of kids and traffic noise, it is very, very hard to develop meditative quiescence. If we are living an active life, or in poor health, or very discouraged, it is difficult to reach meditative quiescence. Many causes and conditions, internal and external, must be brought together in order effectively to develop mental stabilization, and this is true of other practices as well.

But not the Mind Training. This practice comes into its own under precisely such unfavorable conditions. The point, of course, is the transformation of unfavorable circumstances into the path, so that they become aids to our spiritual practice. We don't need to save up our money for a one-year retreat

to do the Mind Training. We don't need a special retreat facility. We don't need a teacher on hand at all times. We don't
even need good health, let alone abundant food, lovely surroundings, and companions. All these things help, but we can
implement the Mind Training in the broadest spectrum of circumstances, without waiting. There is no ground for procrastination in this practice, no way to ever say, "I really want to
practice Mind Training, but first of all I have to. . . ." All circumstances nurture this practice.

Now practice what is most important.

According to Buddhist understanding, our streams of consciousness have no beginning. We have had previous lives, and
lives still previous to those. In many lifetimes we were not even
human beings, and many of our human lifetimes were not conducive to spiritual practice. We lacked spiritual teachers, or
inclination, or opportunity. We made a living, or we died
prematurely, or whatever: we just got by. We could not devote ourselves to eradicating the true sources of suffering and
cultivating awakening. Now, in this present lifetime, we have
the extremely rare circumstance of a fully endowed human life.
We have met all the conditions, internal and external, for an
enormously fruitful and meaningful life. Not only can we increase our contentment in this life, but we can also sow the
seeds for fortunate rebirth in the future, so that we can continue our spiritual practice into the very next lifetime, and the
one after that and one after that. In this way we can develop
some real momentum for spiritual growth. We have before us
the opportunity to sow those seeds and the means to eradicate
mental distortions from their root. It is within our reach to
attain full awakening, and whatever we neglect to do in terms
of spiritual growth in this lifetime is not because of lack of
opportunity but simply because of an inadequacy from our
own side.

We need not take this on faith. Simply look around. People
all around us are striving essentially for the same things that

we are. How many of the five billion people on planet earth, not even counting other sentient beings, are following an effective means to find happiness and truly eradicate suffering at its source? Dharma is an effective means, and we have this rare opportunity.

So now Geshe Chekawa encourages us to practice what is most important. Having encountered something of unutterable value, it would be a staggering loss to shunt it aside and devote our lives to other things as if we had not found such an opportunity. Rather than simply devoting ourselves to mundane happiness that ripens only in this lifetime, let us take into account our welfare in the future lives we are now creating.

The author encourages us to emphasize practice, above all the cultivation of bodhicitta, rather than book learning. As a contemplative himself, he recommends meditation as the most important of all the many ways of cultivating bodhicitta. Finally, rather than relying chiefly on textual information, he encourages us to look to the quintessential guidance of our spiritual mentor.

He makes another point also. Instead of abandoning a certain region as an unsuitable place for practice and going somewhere else, we should apply the antidotes for our own mental distortions wherever we find ourselves. Inner practice is far more important than the outer environment. Having said this in this beautiful region of the eastern Sierras, I would add that where a choice exists, choose the environment that is most conducive to practice.

Do not be contrary.

Sechibuwa gives six examples of different types of contrariness to be avoided.

The first is contrary patience, where we have no patience for any type of discomfort or frustration that comes in the course of our Dharma practice, but plenty of grit and forbearance for protecting our friends and putting down enemies.

The second example is contrary aspiration: not aspiring to

purify the unwholesome imprints from our mind stream, or to collect merit, or to cultivate wisdom, or to transform the mind and heart, but instead aspiring for the so-called bounties of saṃsāra, totally mundane pleasures that are fleeting and essentially unsatisfactory.

The third is contrary experience, where we seek a wide variety of experiences of a totally mundane nature, but do not seek deeper experience in the spiritual domain.

The fourth is contrary compassion, where we feel no sympathy for those who are dominated by the inner sources of suffering, but instead pity those who encounter hardships in their Dharma practice. To put this in context, consider the case of a yogi who has lived in a cave above Dharamsala in northern India for years, practicing very earnestly and with perseverance. When he visited Massachusetts recently, he shared with us some of the experiences he had gone through. He mentioned that for six years in the mountains he had suffered one hardship after another. Hearing this we might be tempted to think, "This poor fellow, living on a bag of rice and beans all year, snowed into a cave for the winter with very poor clothing, and on top of all this, tormented by malignant spirits. If he could only enjoy life like us." But the yogi told us also that after six years he experienced a number of breakthroughs and, as a result, he is now in a continuous state of inexpressible well-being. He had meditated so deeply, he said, that there is virtually no distinction now between his meditation and his post-meditation period.

The point is that most of us are subject to suffering and its causes. We can strive very hard for our own happiness, but without the wisdom of Dharma this aspiration simply leads to more discontent of a wider and wider variety. As long as we fail to apply effective means, we are simply creating more causes for suffering, and the suffering does not run out. This style of life is self-perpetuating and does not cease of its own accord. In contrast, the hardship and disappointments that come in the course of a sound Dharma practice are finite, because we are working to root out the obscurations of our innate Buddha nature. As long as there are so many beings in the world who are suffering and who, as Śāntideva says, are chasing the sources of suffering while destroying the sources of their own happiness, then our compassion is misplaced when we pity a meditator who encounters difficulties while striving to rend the fabric of saṃsāra. Rather let the compassion go to those beings who are not devoting themselves to effective means to fulfill their own aspirations.

The fifth example of contrariness is contrary concern: concerning ourselves not with Dharma practice, but simply with the acquisition of wealth, the protection of loved ones, overcoming our enemies—the affairs of this life that are significant for a day or a year, but have utterly no significance beyond the context of this lifetime.

The final example of contrariness is contrary rejoicing. Instead of rejoicing in the wholesome deeds of other sentient beings, and the virtue of fully enlightened beings, we rejoice in the misfortune that comes to our enemies.

Do not be erratic.

We may practice the Mind Training enthusiastically for a few weeks or months, and then find that we have not yet attained bodhicitta. Feeling that it is not working, we shift to some other kind of practice. When this fails to give us the satisfaction we are looking for, we turn to yet another technique. After doing that for a while, we are dissatisfied and once again give the Mind Training a whirl. After carrying on like this for a while we say, "Fiddlesticks, none of that stuff works; let's go to a movie and forget about the whole business." This type of erratic discontinuity of practice is ineffective. We may give it a lot of effort, but it yields little benefit. This erratic quality can be especially a problem for Western Dharma practitioners: how earnest we can be, and how totally erratic as well! A Tibetan lama once commented that Western Dharma practice is often like taking a shower, then going out all spick and span to roll in some mud, then recognizing how filthy we are, going back into the shower, then going out to roll in the mud again.... A lot of time and effort is expended with very little to show for it.

We may have a fantastic technique, and practice with gusto when we are in a conducive environment such as a meditation course. But if technique is all we have, our practice falls like a house of cards as soon as that supportive environment is missing. What can provide the continuous incentive for maintaining a Dharma practice that is not erratic? More understanding. When Dharma begins to saturate the way we view the world, our attitudes and values, it naturally provides an ongoing impetus for us to apply the techniques we have learned. This wealth of theoretical background for practice is one of the great strong points of Tibetan Buddhism.

Practice decisively.

Before we engage in a practice, we should first of all consider whether we are up to it. Have we fulfilled any necessary prerequisites? Looking at the four preliminaries mentioned at the outset of this Mind Training, for example, we should examine whether we have some foundation there. If not, and if we aspire to this path, then we should work to become familiar with the preliminaries. After this foundation is established, reappraise the practice again. See whether it continues to hold promise, whether it could be effective in bringing about some transformation in our life. Only with this necessary preparation should we begin the practice, and then go into it full-mindedly and with whole heart. With this decisiveness we can carry through patiently and with courage for the long term, and spare ourselves from withdrawing halfway through, thinking we are not really up to this.

Free yourself by means of investigation and analysis.

In this sixteenth practice we are told to investigate and identify our most predominant mental distortion. Are we angry or aggressive? Do we tend to have a lot of attachment, or anxiety, or confusion, or perhaps sheer ignorance? Are jealousy or selfishness major problems? The task is to identify our major source of mental affliction.

The author then directs us to seek out the objects that trigger this mental distortion. Having done so, the opportunity to liberate ourselves from this affliction becomes fertile. When we find ourselves in the type of situation that stimulates our predominant mental distortion, we can be especially aware and very much in the present. We can come like a warrior onto the battle ground, prepared to apply all of our Dharma wisdom to the attenuation and eventual eradication of that mental distortion. If the external situation is overwhelming, and our mental distortions will inevitably overpower our antidotes, it is better to withdraw than to be conquered. If defeat cannot be avoided, then avoid that situation.

Do not be boastful.

The examples that illustrate this seventeenth practice focus on drawing attention to our practice. We may point out some great kindness we have shown to others, of which they may have been unaware. Or we describe how our practice is going so well, the amazing insights we have reached during a retreat, how austere we have been, sleeping just three hours a night. . . . Even if we are accurate, this exaltation of our own greatness is not a sign of mental maturity, but instead pollutes our spiritual practice. Rather than serving as an antidote to mental distortions, this actually feeds our egotism and our sense of superior self-importance.

Do not bind yourself with hatred.

An alternative translation of this eighteenth practice is "Do not retaliate." When someone is insulting, hostile, or just thoughtless to us, this practice entails not retaliating, neither manifestly in actions of body or speech, nor even with our minds. As Śāntideva says, there is no greater austerity than patience. A Dharma practice certainly should be focused on developing this inner fortitude; insofar as we can bear the brunt of others' hostility and aggression, our Dharma practice is acting as an antidote for our self-grasping. Anything that helps us to measure the present level of our self-grasping is to our benefit, and one such measure consists in noting how easily we are insulted. Being easily affronted by others' hostility indicates a strong sense of self-grasping, that surfaces as self-importance or indignation. When a vicious word produces just the slightest flutter but no contorted fist in our hearts, it is a very good sign indeed.

Do not be fickle.

This nineteenth practice does not need much commentary. It especially concerns our relationship with other people. Presenting ourselves to others as a trustworthy friend and then letting them down is being fickle. And being fickle is incompatible with the aspiration of entering into the bodhisattva's way of life.

Do not desire gratitude.

The final practice is also self-explanatory. When we render a service to others we may not hope for a reward as gross as money, or a favor in return, or a state of indebtedness; but we may still linger after the deed is done, as if we have one thread attached, wanting some acknowledgment, some show of gratitude. This is hardly a malignant attitude, and it certainly is very human. But we can do even better. Let the act of kindness be so pure that we derive full satisfaction from the engagement of the deed. And not just eighty percent satisfaction with twenty percent lingering in hopes of gratitude! Pure service simply reaches out without expecting return.

★   ★   ★

This completes the seventh point of the Seven Point Mind Training, and the reflections that I have to offer on the practice. What do we do next? I would recommend going back to the beginning of the text and working through it again; for although our memory may be reasonably good, we probably cannot recall everything that came up in the text. Many elements of this training are new threads for the fabric of our lives; for them to become part of the natural and spontaneous repertoire of living, we need to go over them slowly, again and again.

So we recall the beginning of the text. First of all train in the preliminaries. Gain a deeper and deeper experience of the preciousness of a fully endowed human life. What does that mean? What is the potential of the life that we are now endowed with? What does it mean that this life is both precious and rare, and what are the reasons? The second preliminary was to integrate the fact of our own death, and of impermanence in general, into our daily conscious awareness. Thirdly, meditate on the law of karma, the nature of actions and their results, not only for this lifetime, but for future lifetimes. And finally, consider the faults of saṃsāra, how this self-perpetuating cycle of birth, aging, sickness, and death is dominated by mental distortions. Integrating such awareness into daily life provides the foundation for developing ultimate and relative bodhicitta. And on we go, to the next point.

Here is the version of the verses I prepared for myself:

First things first:
    Precious life,
    death,
action's fruit,
    and suffering.

Training in the bodhicittas:
    Stability first.
    All this is dream.
    Where is unborn awareness?

Even emptiness is empty;
Let it rest in the light.
Now walk in the dream.
Giving and taking,
With every breath.
Objects of attachment, hostility, confusion:
    the poisons are the roots of virtue.
Remember in words.

Turning obstacles into aids:
    Bad times, turn boulders into stepping stones.
    One thing only to blame.
    Kindness, especially to the enemy.
    No reality of its own, but all an emanation of the Buddha.
    Four practices:
        Gather good, make pure the bad,
        thank spirits who bring either.
    Whatever happens, take it in.

Synthesis—five powers, life and death:
    Resolve to achieve the bodhicittas,
    Familiar, constantly close.
White seed of virtue blossoming in life,
        at death releasing attachment.
    Prayer.
Abandoning self-grasping.

The measure of training the mind:
    All Dharma has one goal.
    My self the better witness.
    Rely on the happiness of the mind.

The pledges:
    Three principles:
        Precepts unbroken;
        Be neither ostentatious,
        Nor uneven.

Change yourself but stay the same.
Don't criticize.
Think nothing of the other side.
Don't hope for great results.
Don't eat poisonous conceit.
Don't lean lightly on the pillar of distortion.
No sarcastic words.
No lying in wait for the weak.
No passing the load.
Don't take credit at the top.
No deceit.
Keep the devil away from the divine.
No profit from another's loss.

The practices:
One practice for every situation.
One answer to any withdrawal.
Remember each beginning, each ending.
Patience at either pole.
Promises worth more than life.
Three austerities against distortion:
Antidotes, abandoning, cutting at the root.
Three causes of awakening:
Teaching, understanding, everything in favor.
Three degenerations:
Doubting the Dharma, enthusiasm fading, less concern.
Three never to part with:
Practice in body, speech, and mind.
Attention to the close ones who provoke you.
Don't count on external conditions.
Priorities. Practice what's important.
Upside down and contrary:
Patience for distortion,
aspiring to samsara,
looking wide instead of deep,
pity how hard the path.

Be constant in the practice,
and decisive.
   Investigate and analyze.
No boasting.
No striking back.
No fickleness.
Pure service, without wanting thanks.

Glossary

bardo: the intermediate experience following death and before one's next life.

bodhicitta (pronounced *bodhichitta*): the altruistic aspiration to achieve spiritual awakening for the benefit of all sentient beings.

bodhisattva: a person who is continually motivated by bodhicitta naturally and effortlessly.

devas: gods dwelling in the sensual realm, the realm of form, or the formelss realm.

dharmakāya: literally the "truth body" of a Buddha, meaning the mind of a Buddha.

dharmapālas: mundane and supramundane protectors of the Dharma

guru: spiritual mentor

karma: action, or more specifically, the volition behind an overt action.

lama: the Tibetan translation of the Sanskrit *guru*.

mantra: syllables recited for their spiritually transformative power.

nirmāṇakāya: literally, the "emanation body" of a Buddha, referring to the forms a Buddha takes when appearing to ordinary beings.

nirvāṇa: liberation from cyclic existence.

prāṇāyāma: spiritual exercises, involving the breath, designed to modulate one's vital energies in order to calm and purify one's mind.

sadhana: an integrated meditative practice.

samādhi: meditative concentration.

saṃsāra: cyclic existence, characterized in the case of humans by the cycle of birth, aging, sickness, and death.

sambhogakāya: literally, the "fulfilled body" of a Buddha, referring to the forms a Buddha takes when appearing to other Buddhas and to bodhisattvas who have directly realized ultimate truth.

śūnyatā (pronounced *shunyata*): the emptiness, or sheer absence, of intrinsic existence; a synonym for ultimate truth.

sūtra: a discourse attributed to the Buddha.

svabhāvakāya: literally, the "natural body" of a Buddha, referring to the ultimate nature of a Buddha's mind.

tantra: a class of esoteric teachings and practices in Mahāyāna Buddhism, distinguished from the more exoteric class of the sutras.

yoga: a contemplative practice aimed at spiritual awakening.